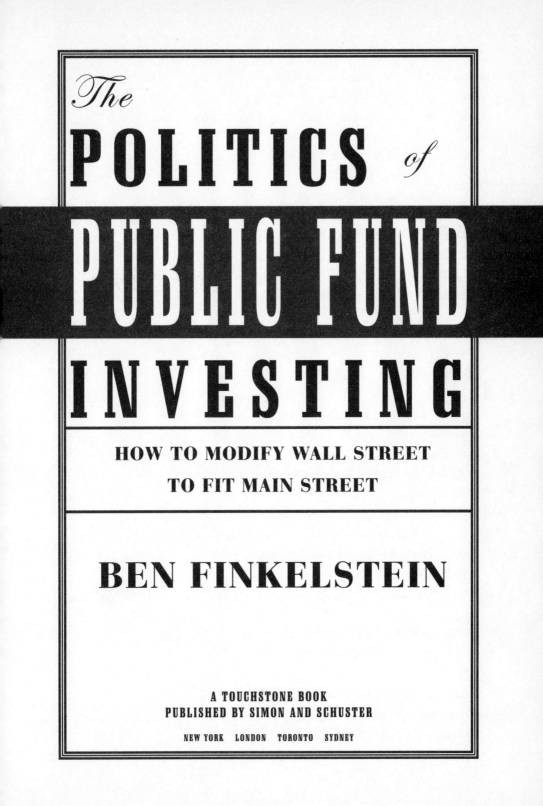

The
POLITICS of
PUBLIC FUND
INVESTING

HOW TO MODIFY WALL STREET
TO FIT MAIN STREET

BEN FINKELSTEIN

A TOUCHSTONE BOOK
PUBLISHED BY SIMON AND SCHUSTER

NEW YORK   LONDON   TORONTO   SYDNEY

SIMON & SCHUSTER
TOUCHSTONE
Rockefeller Center
1230 Avenue of the Americas
New York, NY 10020

SIMON & SCHUSTER and TOUCHSTONE and colophons are registered
trademarks of Simon & Schuster, Inc.

Manufactured in the United States of America

10   9   8   7   6   5   4   3   2   1

Library of Congress Cataloging-in-Publication Data
Finkelstein, Ben.
    The politics of public fund investing : how to modify Wall Street
to fit Main Street / Ben Finkelstein.
        p. cm
    Includes bibliographical references and index.
        1. Investment of public funds—United States.
    2. Local finance—United States.
    HJ3833.F52 2006
    322.67'2520973—dc22   2006042214

ISBN-13: 978-0-7432-6729-8
ISBN-10:   0-7432-6729-X

To Mom and Dad
the source of my life

To my wife
who lights up my life

To my children, Lauren, Chasen, Dustin, Randon, and Daryn,
who keep the light burning

ACKNOWLEDGMENTS

Most books have a single author; this one shares many. The insights gained from conversations and experiences with clients and workshop participants over many years formed the pool of concepts from which this book was created. My role was simply to convert their experiences and ideas into the first comprehensive treatment of how to modify Wall Street methods to fit the Main Street way of investing.

My deepest thanks go to my partner and friend, Neal Willard. His integrity and commitment to educating public fund personnel was an inspiration. Thanks, also, to Kevin Webb, for never letting me forget that sound practice comes only from a sound philosophy.

In addition, special thanks are owed to the outstanding group of practitioners and scholars who acted as an advisory board for this book: Kaye Mirabelli, Kent Rock, Craig Husting, Felicia Landerman, Steve Stark, David Carr, Christine Vuletich, Jerry Rogers, Lisa Strong, Tom Mueller, Kenneth Spray, Rick Phillips, Laura Fitzpatrick, Todd Corbin, Becky Lingad, Ernie O'Dell, Ricki Williams, and Vernon Perry are all practitioners par excellence. Very special thanks go to two academics, Rich Callahan and Elizabeth Keating, for showing me how powerful academia is when this subject is taught with an eye on real world practices. Likewise I am truly grateful for the unique perspectives of Michael Dukakis and Ernest Almonte.

Motivated by an interest in advancing the best practices in our field, these very special people shared their ideas, reviewed drafts of the manuscript, and offered suggestions for improvement. The book has benefited greatly from those suggestions, though as author, I must lay claim to any shortcomings in the final product.

Acknowledgments for their support of my efforts should also be made to my colleagues at the Stanford Group, especially Sandra Ritchie and

Jane Bates, who never wavered in believing this project deserved to be done, and Heidi Battle, who kept me thinking straight. In addition, I would like to thank two firms, Wilshire Associates and Lehman Brothers, for providing analytical and intellectual resources. Finally, my sincerest thanks go to freelance scribe Dick Luecke of Salem, Massachusetts, who provided writing and editorial assistance. Dick probably learned more about public fund investing over the course of this project than he ever cared to know.

BEN FINKELSTEIN
Houston, Texas
January 2006

CONTENTS

Acknowledgments   ix
Foreword   xiii
Preface   xv

PART ONE—MAIN STREET PHILOSOPHY

Chapter 1   WALL STREET VERSUS MAIN STREET   3

Chapter 2   INVESTMENT POLICY AND POLITICS   14

Chapter 3   RELEVANT PERFORMANCE MEASUREMENT   24

Chapter 4   FOUR STEPS TO CREATING A POLITICALLY
             CORRECT PORTFOLIO   35

Chapter 5   OPTIMIZING INCOME AND MINIMIZING RISK   50

PART TWO—TECHNICAL TOOL KIT

Chapter 6   OPPORTUNITY COST   77

Chapter 7   PROFITING FROM LOSSES   90

Chapter 8   UNDERSTANDING AND APPLYING DURATION   107

Chapter 9   CALLABLE SECURITIES   121

Chapter 10   PUBLIC FUND ANALYTICS   144

Glossary   163
Notes   169
Index   173

FOREWORD

Why should you read this book? That is a fair question. The book is a comprehensive and detailed guide. What will you gain? I say plenty. Open your mind, and let me tell you what's in it for you.

As the manager of a public fund for nearly two decades, I understand firsthand the fiduciary responsibility to construct a politically correct portfolio. We must protect taxpayers' dollars, provide for immediate liquidity, and earn a market rate of return. Ultimately, my success in managing the portfolio will provide the optimal budget for services while helping to reduce taxes. This is at the heart of what any public fund seeks to accomplish. Unfortunately, until now there has been no guidebook for winning this game.

Most of us are familiar with the *Wall Street Journal.* But how many of us have read the *Main Street Journal?* Probably none of us, because although there are a multitude of publications geared toward Wall Street investing, those that address the fundamentals of Main Street are rare. There is no *Main Street Journal,* but if there were, I'd be the first to subscribe. Before the appearance of *The Politics of Public Fund Investing,* I knew of no complete resource specific to my field. I cannot count the number of times that I have had to turn to Wall Street publications to gain an understanding of the products and strategies appropriate to managing a fixed-income portfolio. Yes, many of the risks and techniques described in those books and periodicals are relevant to both private fund and public fund investing. But are the risk tolerances the same? Is a particular strategy or investment suitable for a public fund? The answers to these questions and more are found in this book. Finkelstein provides thought-provoking dialogue in this practical guide for working within a framework specific to a public entity.

The Politics of Public Fund Investing is the first of its kind to formally make the distinction between Wall Street and Main Street investing. Although the products, practices, and risks may overlap, the distinction between the two is ever present. Whereas Wall Street focuses on economics and managing return, a public fund is heavily influenced by politics and the need to balance preservation of principal with the mandate to optimize income. This book effectively explains the uniqueness of public funds as it brings to light the subtle issues applicable to their stewardship. By clearly illustrating specific techniques, standards, and procedures, it educates the reader in how to optimize and measure performance. Finkelstein's comprehensive framework is highly reflective of the nuances of a public fund. If you want to delve into the realities of Main Street investing, this book is for you.

I have worked with Ben Finkelstein for many, many years. I consider him to be an expert in the field and a source for Main Street investing. His ideas are innovative and his discussions compelling. His keen understanding of the political environment and how it impacts public investing is remarkably on-target. He has built a successful career based on years of experience, invaluable research, and a strong desire to educate. I highly recommend his book for its clarity and depth of coverage: It is unlike any resource out there.

FELICIA LANDERMAN, Cash and Investment Manager
Palm Beach County Clerk and Comptroller's Office

The Treasurer was just summarizing his formal presentation to the City Council. The city's $18 million reserve fund, he explained, had earned $405,000 over the past fiscal year, a 2.25 percent return. Further, that amount was consistent with budget expectations. "Thanks to this performance," he told his audience, "we were able to meet all scheduled financial obligations, and a few that were both costly and unanticipated, such as the sewer and water lines that had to be rebuilt in the Locust Hill neighborhood.

"As we enter the new fiscal year," he continued, "we do so with a balanced portfolio of two-to-three-year U.S. government agency bonds, short-term U.S. Treasuries, and money-market-like investments in the state pool. Together, these should produce sufficient interest income to meet the fund's budget obligations for the rest of this year."

The Treasurer was pleased with both the fund's performance and his own presentation. He had done everything that was expected of him. The City's funds were safe and intact; all financial obligations for which the fund was responsible had been met on time; and he had produced $405,000 in cash without taking unacceptable risks. "That's almost a half-million dollars that taxpayers won't have to pay," he thought to himself with some satisfaction.

Not everyone in the Council chamber was as pleased as the Treasurer. Harold Steadman, a prospective mayoral candidate, had a few things to say—as usual. "I'm glad to know that the fund administered by the Treasurer has met its budget obligations," Councilor Steadman began. "But a 2.25 percent return doesn't seem like anything to brag about. Consider, for example, that the state pension fund in which we participate had a 6.25

percent return over the same period. One has to wonder why our taxpayers should be satisfied with anything less."

"Well, for starters, we aren't a pension fund," the Treasurer responded. But before he could complete his argument, another councilor rose to speak.

"I'm no accountant," said Councilor Sandoval, holding up the fund's annual report, "but I don't understand how you can say that our funds are safe and intact when these financial statements show losses."

The Councilor was referring to a mark-to-market requirement of the Governmental Accounting Standards Board (GASB 31), which requires entities like the City to reflect the ups and downs of securities markets in their financial statements. The requirement had little impact on day-to-day fund performance, but it created substantial confusion for the laypeople charged with overseeing public funds.

At this point, the Council President recognized a citizen in the gallery who had a question of his own. "I'm not a professional investor," the man said, "but even I know that if you want a respectable return you shouldn't tie up all your money in short-term, low-yielding securities, as we've done here. And as a property owner I know that every dollar that you fail to earn is a dollar I have to pay in taxes. So here's my question: Has the City ever considered putting some of that $18 million into a diversified mutual fund of corporate bonds, dividend-paying utility stocks, and S&P stocks? Most of my 401(k) money is in that type of fund, and I got a 9 percent return this year. Why can't the City do the same?"

The Treasurer wasn't surprised by these questions. After five years on the job he had heard them before. But he knew that answering them quickly and convincingly in this political forum would be difficult. The council members, the citizens in the gallery, and the newspaper reporter over in the corner were all waiting to hear what he had to say.

This council meeting is fictitious, but it is representative of real dramas that play out in cities, counties, water districts, and other public entities around the country. Wherever public monies are invested, the people who do the investing and those who oversee them face similar issues and deal with the same questions:

- Is the public's money being invested safely?
- Will that money be available to meet financial obligations as they come due?
- Can a higher return be obtained without taking imprudent risks?

This book will help you find the right answers. A reader schooled in traditional money management—the Wall Street way—might say, "I already know how to answer those questions." Indeed, it's natural to think that the portfolio-management tools that work so well for individual investors, mutual funds, and even pension funds can be transferred directly to the world of public funds. Those tools were created to help portfolio managers measure risk, risk-adjusted returns, and total returns, and to forecast investment cash flows. But strange things happen when we try to apply traditional money-management techniques on Main Street. We discover that investing isn't simply about economics. Politics and election cycles also matter, and they give notions of safety and expectations of income a different twist. We encounter constraints on how citizens think about our business—constraints that don't apply to Wall Street. For example, following the citizen's recommendation that money be put into mutual funds containing stocks and corporate bonds would violate a public fund's policy, and end the manager's career. Wall Street's favored approaches to evaluating portfolio performance likewise make little sense in the world of public funds.

Because Main Street is so different from Wall Street, it needs its own "textbook of practice." This book aims to fill that need by providing a politically aware framework for creating Main Street investment portfolios, and for managing the perennial tug-of-war between safety of principal and portfolio income. It is based on more than twenty years of training and educating countless public funds staff members, managers, and their supervisors from all across the country.

Traditional textbooks on portfolio-management theory view money management exclusively from a total return perspective, and they encourage the use of market benchmarks in assessing portfolio performance. This book does neither, since neither total return nor market-based performance benchmarks are appropriate in the world of public funds. Instead, it offers both a philosophy and a set of practical tools for creating economic value within a political environment.

WHO SHOULD READ THIS BOOK

The Politics of Public Fund Investing is written for four audiences, and chances are that you are in one of them:

- Individuals who work for or supervise public funds. These include treasurers, financial managers, investment board members, and professional portfolio managers. Generally speaking, these people have limited time, resources, and staff, and their training opportunities are few. This book will give them an in-depth look at how politically acceptable portfolios should be constructed, managed, and reported.
- Elected and appointed public officials—mayors, council members, commissioners, and so forth. They are direct stakeholders of public fund investing.
- Students of public administration and finance—the public officials of tomorrow. This book provides them with a practical perspective on managing taxpayer money.
- Portfolio managers and their overseers at foundations and endowments, and corporate cash managers. They are likewise concerned with safety of principal, liquidity, and income optimization, and they may find useful ideas for addressing those concerns in this book.

HOW THIS BOOK IS ORGANIZED

The book has two parts. Part One, "Main Street Philosophy," is comprised of five chapters that deal with the qualitative, political side of public fund management. They make a case for a unique approach to managing the funds of cities, counties, water districts, and other public entities. They follow through with practical steps you can take to create and manage what we call politically correct portfolios. Everyone who picks up this book should read at least Part One, because it spells out the unique environment of public fund investing and why traditional Wall Street approaches are inappropriate.

Chapter 1 addresses key differences between Wall Street and Main Street, explaining which methods of the former are unsuited to the latter—and why. It also examines the problem of political risk, fund-manager performance appraisal, and the dilemma that confronts every public fund manager: either take some risks to earn higher income or reduce political risk for oneself and one's boss by being more conservative. Politics has a big impact on how people approach those choices. Every public fund operates under general guidelines spelled out in a formal investment policy.

Chapter 2 provides a framework for moving from investment policy (a rule book), to an investment plan (a playbook). It makes an important distinction between what is "legal" in terms of policy and what is "suitable" in terms of the objectives of fund stakeholders. "Suitability" addresses the safety and income requirements of a public fund's stakeholders within the constraints of investment policy.

Chapter 3 is about performance appraisal. Wall Street uses total return and risk-adjusted return to evaluate fund performance. The performance of a public fund, in contrast, is routinely appraised by comparing it to others with which it has little in common. Have you ever heard a comment such as the following? "Our city portfolio earned a 2 percent yield this past year while the state fund yielded 2.7 percent. We must be doing something wrong." In other cases, public funds are often compared to a market benchmark, such as the Merrill Lynch 1–3 Year Government Index. This chapter demonstrates why each of these methods is inappropriate and proposes a more realistic and relevant approach. That new approach provides a superior assessment of fund-manager performance against *all* policy objectives by focusing on fiduciary benchmarks instead of market benchmarks. At the same time it helps fund managers create suitable portfolios that serve the unique interests of the entities that employ them.

With the concepts of "legal" and "suitable" now defined, chapter 4 provides a four-step process for building a "politically correct" portfolio—that is, a portfolio that preserves principal while optimizing income at a level of risk that stakeholders will accept. The first steps of that process call for a liquidity subportfolio structured to meet the cash needs of the fund. This is the best way to assure every fund's number one objective remains principal preservation.

With adequate liquidity and safety of principal assured, the fund manager can move on to a final objective, and the subject of chapter 5: optimizing income within the constraints of acceptable risk. This is an objective that too many Main Street managers fail to achieve, since being extrasafe, even at the expense of taxpayers, is their best assurance of job security. This chapter shows how you can be safe *and* optimize income.

Part Two, "Technical Tool Kit," consists of five chapters that address the quantitative side of public fund management. The first of these, chapter 6, is on opportunity cost. For fund managers, opportunity cost is the money they leave on the table when they fail to optimize the risk/return trade-off. Every dollar left on the table is a dollar of public goods or services that citizens will not receive. This chapter provides a technique for measuring opportunity cost and determining how that cost can best be communicated to public and political bodies.

Chapter 7 explains the paradox of why selling gains and holding losses not only reduce budgets but is, to quote Peter Lynch, "like pulling out the flowers and watering the weeds." Selling gains can make you look like a champ in the short term, but it usually results in having to reinvest at lower rates—making you a chump in the long term. Managers can actually enhance their budgets through periodic portfolio rebalancing that involves the simultaneous and judicious sale of a loss position with the purchase of another security. This chapter explains how to do it.

Chapter 8 tackles the important but difficult concept of duration, and shows how a portfolio manager with limited financial training can use duration to enhance fund performance. Many public funds are utilizing securities with options, particularly callable U.S. Agency debt. This chapter discusses the use of effective duration in managing a portfolio interest rate risk. Higher duration translates into higher price volatility due to interest-rate changes. This yardstick for measuring price volatility is far superior to the measure still used by most managers: average life.

Chapter 9 continues the discussion of duration from the perspective of callable securities. It provides a framework for evaluating the risk/return trade-off between U.S. Agency bullets and callable structures.

Chapter 10 presents a portfolio of tools to help public fund managers apply state-of-the-art analytics to manage portfolio risk and return.

To enhance learning, a glossary of terms that are either unique to public fund management or highly relevant, has been appended to the text. See page 163.

PART ONE

MAIN STREET PHILOSOPHY

CHAPTER 1 =========

Wall Street Versus Main Street

Traditional wisdom can be long on tradition and short on wisdom.

—WARREN BUFFETT

KEY POINTS COVERED IN THIS CHAPTER

- The goals of public fund investing
- The Wall Street approach to investing
- Political risk on Main Street
- The problem of performance evaluation
- The important role of communication

Every year thousands of men and women transact the business of public fund management. They work on behalf of counties, municipalities, school districts, water districts, and other entities of government. In all cases, their objectives are threefold:

1. To safeguard the principal over which they have been granted stewardship.
2. To provide for liquidity—i.e., they must assure there is sufficient cash to meet the needs of the entity.
3. To earn a reasonable market rate of return.

On the surface, this is the same set of goals that most private money managers and personal investors espouse, though not necessarily in the same order. A glance through the "objectives" section of most mutual fund prospectuses will confirm that the goals are similar. This begs the question, Why don't public fund managers (Main Street) operate like their private fund counterparts (Wall Street)? Or to put it another way, Why shouldn't more public nonpension entities hire Wall Street firms to manage their money? This question is often asked by elected officials and by taxpayers when the low annual returns on their public funds are reported. "What? We earned a paltry 2.5 percent when my personal investments earned 8 percent?" The people asking this question often speculate that if their public entities had "more professional management"—the kind they associate with Wall Street—those public entities would be making a lot more money. And more money would help shore up public budgets and take some pressure off taxpayers.

The notion of investing public funds using Wall Street methods has substantial intuitive appeal. After all, isn't public money the same as private money? But the more one understands Main Street's unique requirements, the less appropriate Wall Street methods become. This chapter examines key differences between Wall Street and Main Street, and explains why the methods of the former are unsuited to the latter. It also examines the problem of fund-manager performance appraisal, demonstrating that what is straightforward and simple on Wall Street is just the opposite on Main Street.

THE WALL STREET WAY

Wall Street—the universe of broker-dealers, investment bankers, traders, and money managers—has been the home port of money management for well over a century. Until the 1970s, however, its practices were based more on art than on science. Bonds were simple and straightforward IOUs, with none of the financially engineered twists that are so common in the field of fixed-income securities today. Stocks were considered too risky for pension funds, and managers who invested in stocks for private clients and mutual funds did so with little more than a commonsense notion of diversification. Modern techniques for quantifying the risk of a particular portfolio were not available. This situation changed rapidly in the 1970s as the pioneering theories of several financial economists began to take root on Wall Street.

As described by Peter L. Bernstein in his informative book *Capital*

Ideas, today's financial markets are the result of a recent but obscure revolution that took root in the halls of Ivy rather than in the canyons of Lower Manhattan. Its heroes were a tiny contingent of scholars, most at the very beginning of their careers.[1] Many of those obscure scholars—future Nobel laureates such as Harry Markowitz, James Tobin, Paul Samuelson, and William Sharpe—developed the elements of portfolio theory that virtually all Wall Street practitioners now use to create and manage client portfolios. Optimizing what financial scholars have taught us about the risk return trade-off is at the heart of this new science. On the fixed-income side of the business, money managers are also using risk management tools developed by academics to deal with interest-rate volatility.

THE PROBLEM OF POLITICAL RISK

Wall Street's methods have demonstrated their worth over several decades. So one would naturally think they could be applied directly to the management of public funds, which entails investing solely in fixed-income securities. And why not? Wall Street knows everything it needs to know about the risk and return characteristics of such securities: interest-rate risk, purchasing-power risk, credit risk, and so forth. Its people should be able to harness that knowledge and the tools of portfolio theory to deliver what every state, municipality, sewage and water district, and the like desires most: safety, liquidity, and a competitive market rate of return on capital. Public bodies could then rate the performance of Wall Street's fund managers against traditional benchmarks on a risk-adjusted return, using, for example, the Lehman Brothers U.S. Aggregate Index or the Merrill Lynch 1–3 year Government Index. They could retain the services of the best performers and drop those who produced disappointing results.

There is one problem with this simple and appealing solution. The Wall Street Way does not recognize the political risk with which anyone who manages public funds must contend. The politics of ensuring principal safety and liquidity ahead of income shifts the focus from return to a focus on risk above all. In a nutshell it comes down to this: Wall Street manages returns, Main Street manages risk.

Wall Street includes the concept of political risk in its vocabulary, but its definition is very different from the one applied by Main Street practitioners. To Wall Street, political risk is the possibility of loss associated with political developments, primarily in unsettled parts of the world: revolution, civil unrest, expropriation of foreign-owned assets, state control of key industries, and so forth. In this sense, political risk is simply a subset of economic risk. On Main Street, political risk entails all the bad things that can happen to elected officials and their appointees when they take risks—even reasonable risks—with taxpayer money and come up short. Consider this example:

> Helen manages $100 million for Smithtown, a large city. The City Treasurer is her boss. Prodded by the Mayor and the City Council to seek a higher return (political pressure versus political risk), Helen invested in bonds and notes with longer maturities than usual. Everything was fine with this strategy until two things happened. First, market interest rates rose significantly, reducing the market value of Helen's portfolio. Second, Smithtown was hit by an unanticipated fiscal emergency. At her boss's order Helen sold $40 million worth of bonds prior to maturity, resulting in a $300,000 loss for the City. This piece of bad news was trumpeted in the local press and was used by the Mayor's enemies in the City Council to reap political advantage. Those councilors and segments of the public blamed the Mayor for "losing our hard-earned money" and called for the sacking of both Helen and the City Treasurer.

As this story indicates, political risk on Main Street translates into job risk for public fund managers and elected officials. On Wall Street, occasional poor performance may result in the loss of one or two clients, but life goes on. In contrast, poor performance by a public fund manager can end the manager's career. At a minimum, it can create a community brouhaha and the possibility of civil lawsuits.

THE FUND MANAGER'S DILEMMA

Cases like Helen's are typical, and they underscore the dilemma faced by most public fund managers: either take some risks to earn higher income— usually by extending the average maturity of portfolio holdings and reducing liquidity—or reduce political risk for oneself and one's boss by being more conservative. Our experience indicates that politics has a big impact on how people approach these choices. On Wall Street, earnings or performance legitimately drive investment decisions, but on Main Street, the political issues surrounding the preservation of principal, and sensitivity to public needs in the short and the long term, dominate most of the investment decisions. This would be inappropriate if the sole purpose of playing it safe with the people's money was to preserve one person's job—and not fund principal.

> Henry is the manager of a $20 million fund. He is paid $70,000 plus benefits each year. If playing it safe solely to protect his job resulted in a 1.5 percent reduction in return, the entity whose interests Henry is obliged to put before his own would lose $300,000 in incremental fund revenues each year.

Forgoing $300,000 in fund income to save a job worth $70,000 would be irresponsible if that were the *only* reason for playing it safe. Safety of principal is the primary responsibility of the fund manager, but it is not the only one. The interests of the public must always come before those of the people who serve it. But playing it safe is what the politics of public fund investing often requires. The Wall Street manager—a true maximizer—would likely scoff at this behavior and at the very notion of politically driven investment decisions. But in doing so, he or she would be forgetting that politics is the mechanism through which we resolve public issues—and without apologies. Who should run our public institutions? How should public resources be spent? Which groups will bear the greatest tax burdens and which will carry a lighter load? Will we spend now and pay later, or not? These are all public questions, and all are resolved through politics. How the fund manager should balance the three goals of safety, liquidity, and income is likewise a question that is legitimately addressed through politics and law. Thus, fund managers who fail to modify the Wall Street Way to fit the unique circumstances of Main Street increase political risk within their portfolios.

HOW MANAGERS PLAY THE GAME

All public fund managers must contend with the same goals. They are obliged to preserve principal (safety) because they have a fiduciary obligation to preserve and protect the public funds' principal. They must balance their portfolio maturities to accommodate the entity's liquidity requirements, by, for example, matching some bond or bill maturities with the entity's cash needs at particular times. And they must attempt to produce a reasonable return. Because these goals are mutually exclusive to some degree, each imposes constraints on meeting the others. Thus, maximizing safety of principal reduces the opportunity to maximize income, and vice versa. Investment policies specify which should have priority.

Over the years we have taken an informal survey of our workshop participants to determine how they—Main Street practitioners all—prioritize their goals. Participants are asked to weight the importance assigned to three investment policy objectives. The weights must total 100 percent. How would you respond to this survey?

Safety	____ %
Liquidity	____ %
Income	____ %
Total	**100%**

The results are extremely predictable. It is rare that a group gives a total combined weight less than 80 percent or greater than 95 percent to safety and liquidity. The typical group weights the income goal in a range between 5 percent and 20 percent. Though informal, these surveys underscore the power that safety and liquidity exert over Main Street investment portfolios and strategy—despite the political pressure to optimize income.

The public fund manager's inclination toward safety of principal is supported by the need to reduce political risk and by the language of the overwhelming majority of investment policies. But this clarity of purpose is complicated by the manner in which fund performance is evaluated. Evaluation in many cases is not made with respect to the fund's unique concerns for safety, liquidity, and income, as stated in its investment policy. Instead, politicians, pundits, and critics compare fund performance—often inappropriately—to market benchmarks such as the Merrill Lynch 1–3

Year Government Index, or to funds operated by neighboring communities. Consider this scenario:

> With the cameras rolling, a newsman asks the incumbent mayor of a cash-strapped municipality which is more important to her administration, generating income from public funds or preserving principal. "When we invest the taxpayers' money," the Mayor intones, "principal preservation is our single most important goal. If I can paraphrase Will Rogers, it's not the return *on* the investment that matters, it's the return *of* the investment."

Off camera, and in the company of a more knowledgeable crowd, the same mayor is likely to hear a different set of questions. For example, she might be asked, "How much did the city's portfolio earn and how did its earnings compare to those of surrounding communities?" Comparisons to other communities are appealing to critics who have little experience in money management and performance evaluation—a description that fits most elected officials and media editorialists. Such critics fail to realize that comparing the investment performance of different government entities is like comparing apples and oranges. Consider this example:

> Chester, population 60,000, lies on one side of the Mill River. It is a "mature" community in the sense that its population is stable and aging very slightly each year. Consequently, Chester has no forecasted need for new schools or expanded public services. And since most land within the city has been developed, demands for road building, water and sewer lines, and other infrastructure work are minimal. Chester's revenue picture is equally stable; a steady and reliable tax base makes budgeting easy. With no major expenditures on the horizon, and few likely to appear, Chester has decided to allocate more funds than usual to fixed-income securities with three- to five-year maturities. Says the City Treasurer, "Since we have no immediate needs for our public funds, we have sought the higher returns offered by those longer-term investments. Last year, we earned 3 percent. That higher return will help us fulfill the mayor's pledge to stabilize property taxes."
>
> Newfield is located directly across the Mill River from Chester. Unlike its more settled neighbor, Newfield is a young, growing community. Several tract housing and shopping areas have been built in the past

five years, and more are on the planning boards. This growth has broad-ened the town's tax base but has also increased the demand for schools, roads and sidewalks, water and sewer lines, and social services. "Given the situation, we need liquidity," says Newfield's fund manager. "There's no telling when we may have to tap our funds." The town's liquidity needs have forced it to invest in very short-term securities, reducing returns to 2 percent, but assuring that Newfield will not take a loss if securities must be sold prior to maturity.

Chester and Newfield are very different communities, and each has different priorities for its fund investments. Though Chester earns a much higher return than neighboring Newfield, both fund managers are success-ful in doing what is "right" for their communities. Unfortunately, some people in Newfield complain that their fund manager is doing a terrible job. "Just look at Chester's return," they argue. "It's 50 percent higher than ours. Fifty percent!"

This little story demonstrates the perils that Main Street fund man-agers face when performance is evaluated. Evaluation is important, but comparing the performance of one fund manager to that of another without considering the priorities and constraints each faces is bound to produce a false indicator of success or failure. Wall Street fund managers don't have this problem. The field of mutual fund investing is a prime example. Here, funds can be compared on the basis of clearly stated objectives: growth, growth and income, income, and so forth. Direct comparisons are both pos-sible and appropriate. Unfortunately, no comparable standard of public fund performance exists. Consequently, fund managers like the one in New-field have their performance compared with counterparts in much different communities. One aim of this book is to offer a method of performance appraisal that is appropriate for public funds. We'll take that up later.

THE ISSUE OF VOLATILITY

Public fund performance is further complicated by the issue of volatility. Volatility refers to the ups and downs of portfolio value over time. Volatility is the first cousin of price risk, and elected officials don't like it. To better appreciate the role of volatility in the life of fund managers, consider two different public funds, labeled Portfolio A and Portfolio B in Exhibit 1-1.

EXHIBIT 1-1
TWO FUNDS COMPARED

	Initial Investment	Value after 2 Years
Portfolio A	$1,000,000	$1,160,000
Portfolio B	$1,000,000	$1,200,000

The performance reflects what two fund managers have accomplished over a two-year holding period. Each manager began with $1 million to invest. Manager A earned $160,000 in income plus the return of the original $1 million. Manager B did somewhat better, earning $200,000 in income plus the return of the fund's original investment. All investments made by the two managers were within state guidelines. If asked to judge which manager did the better job, and given no other information, the rational observer would cast a vote for Manager B, who earned the higher return.

Now let's add more information about these managers. Manager A followed a passive strategy, which produced minor budget volatility, as shown in Exhibit 1-2. Manager B, in sharp contrast, followed a strategy of active trading.

EXHIBIT 1-2
VOLATILITY AND STRATEGY DIFFERENCES

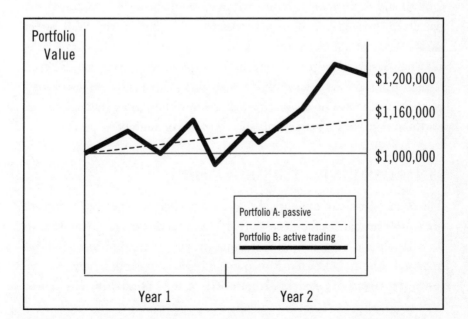

Manager B clearly produced the greater gain in portfolio value, ending the two-year period $40,000 ahead of the other manager. But while Portfolio A increased in value on a predictable and stable basis, Portfolio B was all over the map, its value rising and falling sharply with market conditions. Portfolio B finished ahead, but surely with some heart-stopping moments for the manager and for public officials. The question is, How many fund councils would tolerate this degree of budget volatility? (As we'll see later, Governmental Accounting Standards Board Statement No. 31 unnecessarily injects this kind of market volatility into the budget process.)

What would have happened if Manager B had had to liquidate near the end of year 1—when fund value was underwater—in order to meet some unforeseen fiscal crisis?

As much as public officials and taxpayers would prefer the greater value produced by Portfolio B, it's doubtful that many—if any—would stomach the ups and downs that are the by-product of the trading strategy it represents. Yet those same people will compare the modest gains of their own fund managers with the greater gains of some other fund and complain, "Our people didn't do a very good job." They will be seduced by the final return without ever inquiring about the risks taken to earn it. And make no mistake, volatility in the world of finance is just another name for risk. This is one of the great Wall Street lessons that Main Street folk need to learn. One should never look at return without simultaneously considering the risks taken to get it. The two are inseparable. This is why Wall Street analysts evaluate fund returns on a "risk-adjusted" basis. Thus, on a risk-adjusted basis, Manager A may have outperformed Manager B, even though Manager A's total return was smaller. This is how our workshop participants see it. The majority prefer the lower but more stable return of Portfolio A to the higher yet volatile return of Portfolio B.

THE COMMUNICATION SOLUTION

The related problems of political risk and fund performance evaluation are not simply headaches for elected officials and fund managers who want to do what's best for the entities that employ them. These problems also lead to poor decisions. Political risk encourages behaviors that don't always serve the best interests of taxpayers. It induces a state of mind driven by fear of incurring a reported but unrealized loss. Being supersafe, however, carries no formal penalty. The result is that many managers avoid political risk by accepting too low a return. Inappropriate performance measures create another set of problems, as managers worry that their performance will be compared to funds that operate with very different goals and constraints.

Our own survey data underscore how political pressure and mis-guided performance evaluation pull decision makers in different directions. This dilemma creates a compelling case for a portfolio-reporting and performance-measurement framework that is relevant for Main Street. We'll get to that relevant framework shortly, in chapter 3. Nevertheless, it is absolutely critical that a public fund manager be able to effectively communicate the logic and strategy underlying the operations of the fund. And the starting point of that logic and strategy is found in the investment policy, the subject of our next chapter.

POINTS TO REMEMBER

- Wall Street's investing approach does not take into account the political issues with which public funds must contend.
- Main Street's investment priorities are safety of principal first and foremost, followed by liquidity and income.
- A Wall Street manager's performance can justifiably be assessed against a market benchmark. Such benchmarks are not appropriate for public funds.
- Many public fund managers find themselves under pressure to deliver two seemingly contrary values: safety of principal and higher income.

CHAPTER 2

Investment Policy and Politics

Never mistake motion for action.

—ERNEST HEMINGWAY

KEY POINTS COVERED IN THIS CHAPTER

- The purpose and practical limitations of investment policy
- Making the transition from the investment policy, to the investment plan, to a real portfolio
- How liquidity helps assure safety of principal

Every important and successful human activity operates with two different sets of guidelines, one general and one specific. In managing our households and personal investments we think big thoughts about what we'd like our future to look like: the mortgage paid off before retirement, the children educated, and the nest egg for retirement. We also think smaller thoughts about the specific things we will do to move ourselves closer to that future. Public fund investors must do something very similar, and this chapter spells it out in terms of policies, plans, and priorities.

A FRAMEWORK FOR INVESTING

Presidents, government departments, corporate boards, and foundations all make use of formal policies to define their goals and the approved procedures for reaching them. Generally, the policies are broadly stated and nonprescriptive. For example, the policy of the Federal Reserve is to manage the U.S. money supply in ways that support economic growth and full employment, and to keep inflation under control. Specific directions on how Fed personnel should approach those goals, or how they should prioritize their efforts, are neither stated nor implied in Fed policy.

Policy is also commonplace in the worlds of private and public investment management. In a book written for private money managers, James P. Owen defined an investment policy as

> a written statement of the goals for the portfolio and the rules to be followed by money managers to achieve those goals. It establishes a target rate of return, guidelines for the amount of risk managers may accept in pursuit of the target, and any other restrictions by which managers must abide.[1]

Addressing the same Wall Street audience, Charles Ellis has described investment policy as the foundation on which actual portfolios should be constructed, and how they should be managed over time and through changing market cycles. The purpose of policy, he wrote, is "to establish useful guidelines for investment managers that are *genuinely appropriate* to the realities both of the client's objectives and the realities of the investment and the markets" (italics added).[2] The italicized phrase in this last sentence is particularly important. Policy makers must recognize that what they have written in stone must apply to a world in which change is inevitable.

While Owen and Ellis direct their advice to private money managers, public entities have more recently seen the wisdom of investing within the framework of written policies. Orange County, California's $1.6 billion debacle in late 1994, spurred this interest. Public officials felt that having policies would immunize them from similar fiascos; in this they were partially correct.

Today, both the Government Finance Officers Association (GFOA) and the Association of Public Treasurers of the United States and Canada (formerly Municipal Treasurers Association of the United States and Canada) provide prototypes from which public entities can craft investment policies that meet their unique needs. These prototypes typically contain the following elements:

- A statement of investment objectives
- Statutorily permitted and prohibited financial instruments, including any "legal list"
- Acceptable maturities of fixed-income securities
- A listing of persons having investing authority and responsibility
- A broad description of investment strategies, such as buy-and-hold and active management
- A statement on diversification requirements

Simply having a policy is a step in the right direction for Main Street investors *if* the policy provides a clear, realistic set of parameters and goals. But as we learned in the previous chapter, nonpolicy pressures may infringe on the manager's ability to follow the policy. The person attempting to follow the policy, unlike his Wall Street counterpart, faces the ever-present political problem of having his or her performance evaluated in terms of criteria that have nothing to do with the investment policy. For example, while the policy may insist on safety above all else, the fund manager's performance may be judged on the fund's return relative to one or another market benchmark that does not make safety a top priority.

FROM RULE BOOK TO PLAYBOOK

Even if an investment policy is clear, realistic, and internally consistent, it is nothing more than a "rule book" for playing the game. Like the rule book that governs the sport of football, investment policy indicates what is permitted and what constitutes an infraction. Knowing the rules is essential if you are a coach or a player, but neither they nor an investment manager can play—and win—following the rule book alone. Why not? After all, one entity's investment policy is not much different from that of others with respect to fundamental goals: safety of principal, liquidity, and income. City X's investment policy differs little from City Y's in these key respects.

Further, the rules (policy) stay the same from year to year, even as the world changes around them.

- The economic climate changes from year to year: cities, counties, and other public entities see their revenues and their budgets go up and down.
- Elections bring in a new cast of officials and appointees, people with different spending plans.
- Every entity has unique financial needs.

Something else is required in order to play and win the investment game, some mechanism for adapting policy to the political context—namely, a "playbook."

The fund manager's playbook is a written investment plan, something that very few public fund managers have. Even though many have plans in their heads, almost none have them in written form. A plan should assure several things:

- Adequate liquidity to meet current obligations
- A strategy for optimizing income without violating the risk constraints of the policy
- A diversified portfolio
- Ownership of legal securities

The plan translates the generalities of the policy in specific intentions. For instance, policy may say that you can have from zero to 100 percent invested in U.S. Treasuries; the plan shows the allocation for the current year, say, 70 percent.

The investment plan contains the strategy and tactics required to win the game—that is, how the fund's assets should be invested at any given point in time in a manner consistent with the entity's investment policy. The plan, in effect, acts as a bridge between the investment policy and the dynamic and unique situation faced by the individual who makes day-to-day investment decisions. In addition, the plan incorporates all of the political and fiscal issues that affect the fund manager's job at a given point in time. Exhibit 2-1 on the following page describes the essential differences between an investment policy and an investment plan.

EXHIBIT 2-1
POLICY VERSUS PLAN

Investment Policy (Rule Book)	Investment Plan (Playbook)
A primary document	Is subordinate to the policy document
Defined only in words	Demonstrated by an actual portfolio
General	Specific
Static	Dynamic
Cannot be marked to market	Marked to market
Not related to cash flow	Source of actual cash flow
Incapable of paying obligations	Designed to pay obligations as they come due
Defines political and fiscal issues	Incorporates political and current fiscal issues that affect the fund manager's job, as well as the expectations of key stakeholders
Defines what is legal in terms of levels of risk, final maturity, liquidity minimum, types of investments	Creates what is a suitable portfolio interpretation of investment policy
Determined through assessment of fiscal, political, and practical needs of the community	Bridges the gap between policy constraints and daily changes in financial, operational, and market dynamics

Because investment markets and the entity's financial situation are both dynamic, the investment plan must be:

- Realistic: It recognizes market realities and the liquidity requirements of the entity.
- Dynamic: It is capable of changing in response to market conditions and the financial needs of the entity.

To complete our sports analogy, then, investment policy is the rule book; the investment plan is the playbook; and the strategy behind the tactics of buying and selling portfolio assets is the game in progress. Exhibit 2-2 represents the relationship of these three elements of public fund management. The investment plan converts the investment policy into a working model portfolio. The portfolio plan model reflects what a suitable portfolio should represent. The plan is the vital link between policy and what goes on in the portfolio from day to day. Like a referee, it blows the whistle when performance is poor *and* whenever the players are violating the rules.

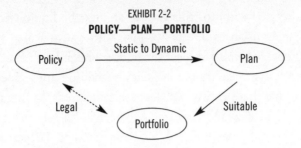

EXHIBIT 2-2
POLICY—PLAN—PORTFOLIO

The logic of developing a plan within the general rules of the investment policy is straightforward. So too is the idea of using the plan to construct an actual portfolio of financial assets that meets policy rules. **The investment plan provides a critical distinction between what is a legal portfolio as defined by investment policy and what is a suitable portfolio as defined by investment actions.** What confounds this straightforward logic is the dilemma described in the previous chapter, in which the sacrosanct pecking order of policy goals—safety, liquidity, and income, in that order—is in conflict with political pressures on fund performance and management. We describe that dilemma here in terms of what is "legal" and what is "suitable."

WHY A POLICY IS NOT A PLAN

Perhaps the biggest problem that managers experience in translating their investment policies into practical plans for creating and managing portfolios is the difference between what is legal in terms of the policy, and what is suitable given the needs and political realities of the entity served by the fund manager.[3] The politics of the job and the realities of financial markets determine what is suitable; in most cases this means an emphasis on liquidity and income. For example, new state fire codes may require a city to build one additional fire station over the next twelve months. Cash must be available as the construction company hits milestones on the building schedule. Judicious attention to liquidity in the investment plan makes this possible. The fund's policy, on the other hand, makes no specific accommodation for the fire station. In Exhibit 2-3, on the following page, we see how the policy describes this city's allowable liquidity and asset percentages in general terms ("Up to 100 percent"). This does not help the fund manager, who must consider payments for this facility among the liquidity needs. The fund manager translates these policy generalities into a plan that can be monitored, reported, *and* can meet the budget obligations.

This investment plan translates policy generalities into a specific representation of what this entity would deem suitable. Let's say that in a normal year, a suitable plan would allocate 20 percent of assets to liquidity, like a state pool with 10 percent to U.S. Treasuries and 70 percent to U.S. Agencies. Further, the portfolio's duration (or interest-rate risk) would be pegged at or near the 2-year U.S. Treasury Note. Each of these allocations is within the constraints of the investment policy and deemed suitable by the fund's supervisors. But this is not a normal year for this city; it has a fire station to pay for. And so the fund manager makes some adjustments as he builds his portfolio, allocating more to liquidity in anticipation of the bills that will be coming from the construction of the fire station. Notice in the exhibit, however, that his portfolio choices remain within the constraints of policy. Next year, after the fire station is paid for, the manager will surely reconfigure the portfolio in a manner that addresses the financial issues of the moment, still within the constraints of policy.

A thoughtfully developed investment plan is flexible and accountable for investment decisions. **It also provides an early warning system for supervisors, should the portfolio drift too far from policy parameters.** The plan becomes the policy shoreline for suitability. Rarely, however, will or should the actual portfolio match the investment plan.

EXHIBIT 2-3
POLICY (LEGAL) VERSUS PORTFOLIO (SUITABLE)

	Policy	Plan	Portfolio	Comment
Liquidity	Up to 100%	20%	40%	Note liquidity is higher due to the construction draws
U.S. Treasury Notes (USTN)	Up to 100%	10%	0%	Reduced Treasury allocation to offset loss of income from holding higher liquidity
U.S. Agencies	Up to 70%	60%	70%	Increased agency allocation to offset higher-than-normal liquidity levels
Duration	2-year	1.7-year	1.2-year	Duration below levels due to excess liquidity needed for construction draw

THE GREATEST RISK

In their breathless pursuit of safety, too many fund managers ignore the greatest risk to principal preservation: insufficient liquidity. Instead, they fixate on default risk, and deal with it through diversification and the purchase of securities with the highest credit ratings (but the lowest yields). The record shows, however, that defaults rarely play a significant role in public fund performance. It is the premature liquidation of a bond below book price that creates loss of principal and puts the fund manager in the hot seat. So take a good look at your portfolio's liquidity position. Then ask yourself: "Which is more likely to occur, a default on one of our U.S. Agency bonds or the premature sale of a security to meet an unexpected obligation?" Most experienced fund managers would say that the premature sale is much more likely. Nevertheless, virtually every investment policy makes liquidity secondary to safety of principal.

TWO DIFFERENT MEANINGS OF LIQUIDITY

As defined by Wall Street, *liquidity* is a measure of the ease with which an asset can be converted into cash. In financial markets, liquidity refers to supply of and demand for a particular security or securities in general. The larger the issue size and higher the credit rating, the larger the universe of buyers. And the more buyers, the better (tighter) the bid/offer spread of the security. Conversely, a bond for which there is little active demand will usually have a wider bid/offer spread. The wider the bid/offer spread, the less liquid or higher the transaction cost of the security. For example, a thousand-share block of General Electric stock is highly liquid; it can be sold in a twinkling very near the posted asking price because there are always buyers in the market. A City of Sandytown Water District bond, in contrast, is much less liquid; chances are that few or no buyers are standing by.

Main Street understands this market-based definition of liquidity, but it also understands and lives with another. To Main Street, liquidity is the ability to meet financial obligations—planned and unplanned—as they present themselves, without having to sell a portfolio security at a principal loss.

Many investors, including inexperienced public fund managers, make the mistake of believing that their principal is safe as long as they invest in U.S. Treasuries, which are default-free for all practical purposes. Unfortunately, the safety ascribed to Treasuries relates only to their default risk, merely one aspect of risk. Rising interest rates can depress the market value of these seemingly risk-free debt instruments as much as those of other fixed-rate IOUs, irrespective of issuer. The longer their maturities and the greater the market interest rate change, the more their market value will decrease.

CREATING A SUITABLE PORTFOLIO

The practical question in the foregoing discussion is this: How can a manager insure that investment practice follows investment policy? In other words, how can a steward of public funds create a portfolio that respects the goals and constraints dictated by investment policy, while recognizing political and market realities—a suitable portfolio? The answer is to interpret the policy through political lenses. In most cases, this means reordering priorities from safety, liquidity, and income to liquidity, income, and safety, as shown in Exhibit 2-4. What? Put safety at the bottom of the list of priorities? On the surface, this sounds heretical and seems a surefire way to lose one's job as fund manager.

EXHIBIT 2-4
A SUITABLE REORDERING OF PRIORITIES

Policy Objectives	Plan Priorities
1. Safety	1. Liquidity
2. Liquidity	2. Income
3. Income	3. Safety

Paradoxically, making liquidity the top-ranked priority usually provides the greatest assurance that principal will be safe. Said another way: *Sufficient liquidity (the highest priority of the investment plan) at the portfolio level is needed to ensure principal preservation (the foremost objective of the investment policy).* This approach makes the portfolio both legal *and* suitable. Here are two reasons why:

1. Maintaining liquidity neutralizes the most common source of principal loss: having to sell bonds prior to maturity in order to meet an unanticipated financial obligation.
2. Default (or credit) risk, the lesser form of risk to principal, can prudently be handled through diversification.

Assuring liquidity while managing a modest amount of default risk through diversification and other means is almost always the most prudent approach to fulfilling one's fiduciary responsibility for safety. It helps the fund manager produce a portfolio that is, again quoting Charles Ellis, "genuinely appropriate to the realities both of the client's objectives and the realities of the investment and the markets."

But putting liquidity first does nothing to solve the political demand to optimize income. Some people are bound to complain, "Our fund's return is less than that of our neighboring community." How should fund managers and fund stakeholders deal with this complaint? The answer is that each fund must interpret its policy in terms of its unique political situation. Two communities with identical rule books (investment policies) will very likely have different playbooks (investment plans). Thus, suitability is the standard by which portfolio performance should be measured. The next chapter elaborates on this solution.

POINTS TO REMEMBER

- Investment policies are not investment plans.
- Investment policy is the portfolio manager's rule book. It identifies goals and the rules to follow to achieve them. A thoughtful policy recognizes the realities of the entity's objectives and the market (per Charles Ellis).
- The investment plan is the manager's playbook. It connects what is legal at a policy level to what is suitable at the portfolio level.
- Managers need both a rule book and a playbook.
- A legal portfolio does not insure it is a suitable portfolio.
- The greatest danger to safety of principal in most cases is insufficient liquidity (i.e., having to sell a bond at a loss prior to maturity to meet an obligation), not risk of default. Thus the best course to safety is to assure adequate liquidity.

CHAPTER 3

Relevant Performance Measurement

Even a stopped clock is right twice a day. After some years, it can boast a long series of success.

—MARIE VON EBNER-ESCHENBACH

KEY POINTS COVERED IN THIS CHAPTER

- Why total return is an inappropriate measure of fund performance
- The importance of measuring performance on the three key dimensions: safety, liquidity, and income
- Suitability as the key to performance appraisal
- The Five *We*'s of suitability

It's not easy being a public fund manager. The investment policies that mandate manager behavior insist on safety of principal, yet stakeholders clamor for higher income. "We are facing major water line repairs this year and need all the money we can get."

Investment earnings are routinely compared to those of other communities with which they have little in common. "How come the City of Willowdale made 2.25 percent on its funds this year while we got a measly 1.5 percent? Maybe we need someone with more investment sense."

When fund performance isn't being compared to that of other communities, it is compared to a one-size-fits-all market benchmark, such as the Merrill Lynch 1–3 Year Government Index, which has no bearing on the liquidity and safety concerns of individual public entities. "Our people can't even get the fund to match a market index. What are we paying them for?"

For many public entities, substantial amounts must be held in highly liquid, low-yielding securities to pay current obligations and protect against the possibility of unbudgeted fiscal emergencies. The alternative is to invest long and risk the possibility of principal loss if bonds must be sold prior to maturity—an even more unacceptable outcome. Doing so would put the fund manager at odds with the rule book of investment policy, which places safety of principal on the highest pedestal.

Given these challenges, more than a few public fund managers find themselves caught between a rock and a hard place with respect to performance measurement. The cause of this unfortunate and unnecessary situation is a flawed approach, one that confounds the people charged with managing public funds and, in many cases, one that creates conflict between fulfillment of the investment policy and the objective appraisal of fund managers.

This chapter examines current practices of performance management and proposes a more realistic and relevant approach. This new approach produces a win-win situation: It helps public entities better assess the performance of their managers against *all* policy objectives, and it helps fund managers create suitable portfolios that serve the unique interests of the entities that employ them. More specifically, this chapter:

- Demonstrates the shortcomings of using total return to appraise fund performance
- Recommends a performance standard that addresses *all* the investment policy objectives of Main Street—a standard that measures compliance of portfolio to policy and helps supervisors identify problems before they occur, not after it's too late to fix them
- Proposes a fiduciary benchmark to replace the traditional market benchmark

WHAT'S WRONG WITH CURRENT PERFORMANCE MEASUREMENT?

There are plenty of good things about being a Wall Street money manager. The pay is excellent, huge bonuses are possible (if not likely), and firms don't cut corners when it comes to providing nice office space, generous expense accounts, and other perks. A manager with a hot hand enjoys many opportunities for public recognition through *Barron's, Forbes,* and television's many money-talk shows. Even a failed Wall Street money manager can count on an exit package that's big enough to finance a new life in retirement or in another business.

Perhaps the best thing about the Street, however, is that its money managers know exactly how their performance will be measured. There is no ambiguity on this score and no hidden agenda. It all comes down to *total return,* which for any time period can be measured accurately with readily available data:

$$\text{Total return} = \frac{(\text{Ending market value} + \text{Income}) - \text{Beginning market value}}{\text{Beginning market value}}$$

This measure is clear and indisputable. Manager and client can discuss performance in terms of this measure. One manager's performance can be compared to that of his or her peers who run similar funds with similar objectives. Indeed, the world of private money managers worships at the Temple of Total Return.

Now consider the world of public fund management. Public fund managers, in contrast to their private counterparts, have no uniform standard of performance. Managers are wisely advised by the GFOA that the portfolio "should obtain a market average rate of return through budget and economic cycles" and that a series of appropriate benchmarks should be established "against which portfolio performance shall be compared on a regular basis." But which market average return does this mean? Short term? Intermediate term? Long term? Should the return on risk-free Treasuries or riskier agency bonds be the standard? Which benchmarks are appropriate? On these questions the GFOA recommendations for the most part are silent, recognizing that each public fund is unique.

The fact is that public funds lack a universal standard of performance. Some jurisdictions may use a market index with maturity and risk characteristics comparable with those of their own portfolios (if such comparisons are even feasible); others link performance to the performance of their state or local government investment pools. In each case, these external benchmarks may have very little to do with what is suitable for the individual fund. Consider this example:

Cheryl manages a public fund that has, for internal reasons (risk of a multimillion-dollar lawsuit with an unfavorable settlement), found it necessary to keep the portfolio's duration or interest-rate risk shorter than the established Merrill Lynch Government 1–3 Year benchmark. Because of this and other circumstances, the portfolio's annual return or purchase yield is 2 percent. Contrast this performance with the index's total return performance of 2.6 percent and Cheryl's portfolio appears to have underperformed the benchmark.

Does this comparison reflect a true and relevant measure of Cheryl's portfolio performance?

Despite the absence of a uniform standard of fund performance, people nevertheless feel compelled to compare themselves or those they supervise to something. It's almost human nature. When they play golf, they compare their scores to the par rating of the course. When they go fishing, they compare the size of their catches to those of other fishermen. So when an internally managed fund asks "How are we doing?" it usually compares the purchase yield of its portfolio to the total return of some external index. But there is no agreed standard for reporting a portfolio's yield. They can use total return, effective yield, or purchase yield, to name a few, but there is no standard. Worse, these yield comparisons overlook the issue of suitability. They deal strictly with the quantitative side of portfolio management while failing to account for qualitative issues that make fund management so interesting and challenging.

If you are managing a public fund, ask yourself, "If I created a portfolio that exactly replicated the Merrill Lynch 1–3 Year Government Index, would that portfolio be suitable given our requirements for safety and liquidity?" Per the investment policy mandate to not speculate, combined with the need to produce stable income, short-term price changes in market indexes like the Merrill Lynch 1–3 Year rarely influence a public fund's investment strategy or budget. So in most cases, the answers would be no. Now ask the same question with respect to any other public fund in your area. And again, the answer would be "no" because every city, county, and school district has different needs and different risk tolerances.

The remedy to this performance measurement problem is for each fund to establish its own standard based on suitability.

CREATING A NEW PERFORMANCE STANDARD

Suitability is the one standard capable of specifying the performance measures appropriate to individual funds. But how can a fund establish that standard? We approach this question through "The Five *We*'s of Suitability":

- We have enough *liquidity* to pay financial obligations as they come due.
- We have an appropriate level of *interest-rate risk*.
- We have a *diversified* portfolio.
- We have only *legal* investments.
- We have an appropriate *market rate of return*.

Any fund manager who can state each of these affirmatively has established a portfolio that meets the standard of both suitability *and* performance unique to his or her fund. What is going on in the town across the river or within some market index is irrelevant. Let's consider each of the Five We's in greater detail.

Liquidity

Liquidity means that the manager can tap the fund in order to meet financial obligations as they come due. Cash is the most liquid portfolio asset. U.S. Treasuries are also highly liquid in the sense that there is an active market of buyers and sellers in the secondary market. However, having to sell a Treasury or other security prior to its maturity could result in a loss of principal, violating the standard of safety. Thus, suitability on this dimension requires that a fund have cash or cash-equivalent assets *sufficient to meet all anticipated obligations* in a timely way. Because liquid assets earn little return, however, liquidity needs to be carefully managed. This can be accomplished by determining liquidity requirement *before* any portfolio assets are acquired. Further, liquidity requirements should be reviewed periodically.

Interest-Rate Risk

Even the most creditworthy bonds are subject to interest-rate risk—that is, the market value of existing bonds declines when prevailing interest rates increase. Any fund that holds bills, bonds, or notes with maturities greater than 30 days lives with this fact of life. A fund is suitable on this dimension of performance when the risk assumed is appropriate.

There is also the problem of volatility, which in the world of finance is another way to describe risk. To appreciate the volatility issue, consider two funds, each under a different manager. Over a number of years, each fund has produced the same average annual rate of return, 3 percent. On the surface, we'd say the managers of these funds turned in equal performances. But take a look at Exhibit 3-1, which maps the performance of the two funds over that period of time. Though each achieved the same average annual return, Manager A's performance was highly volatile. In some quarters he did extremely well; in others he was in net loss territory. Manager B, on the other hand, delivered a much more stable return over the same period. In the language of statistics, we'd say that Manager B's work resulted in very little variance from the mean (average).[1] Which manager would you rather have handling your money? Most people would prefer B, who delivered the same return without the sleep-robbing volatility—that is, without the risk.

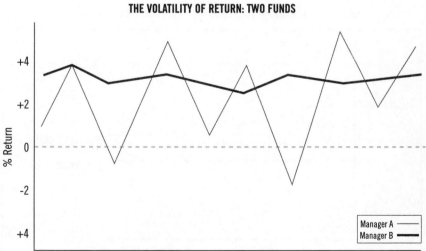

EXHIBIT 3-1
THE VOLATILITY OF RETURN: TWO FUNDS

Diversification

Every experienced investor understands the danger of investing too many portfolio assets in a single maturity, issue, or geographic region. Nor is it a good idea to allow a single securities dealer or bank to handle all fund business; a fiscal crisis at that dealer or bank could hamstring the fund's normal operations.

The worst part of lack of diversification is that it creates risk with no off-setting benefit. In contrast, diversification reduces risk at no loss of return—a phenomenon referred to as the investor's "free lunch." To appreciate this fact, consider Exhibit 3-2, which indicates two layers of risk: systematic risk and nonsystematic risk. Systematic risk is the risk associated with the general market, or "system," of which one's securities are a part. A bond is an element of the bond market and incorporates its particular risk, such as the value swings associated with interest rate changes. Systematic risk cannot be reduced through diversification. Nonsystematic risk, however, is the risk associated with a particular security. For a bond, that usually means default risk. This nonsystematic risk can be reduced through diversification—and without any loss of return if the degree of diversification is adequate. Thus, in the exhibit, systematic risk remains the same, but total risk decreases as more securities are added to the portfolio, and without loss of return.

EXHIBIT 3-2
RISK REDUCTION THROUGH DIVERSIFICATION

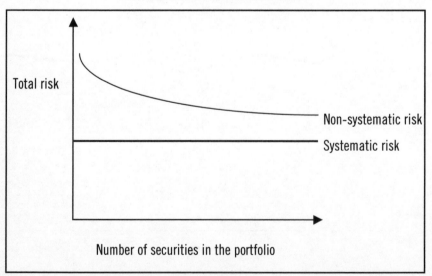

Total risk

Non-systematic risk

Systematic risk

Number of securities in the portfolio

Suitable diversification of a public fund should focus on two critical measures: liquidity and individual holdings. More specifically:

- State pools should not be the only source of primary liquidity.
- Individual security holdings should not exceed a certain percent of portfolio market value, usually defined by policy.
- Individual corporate issuers other than federal agencies should not exceed the policy level percent of portfolio holdings.

Legality

We've said before that not everything that is legal is necessarily suitable. However, a suitable portfolio must be *legal* in the sense that it must conform to investment policy. That is, the playbook must adhere to the rule book. Thus, the public fund must be able to demonstrate that its holdings conform to its investment policy and law as to issuers, maturities, and structure.

Appropriate Market Rate of Return

As described earlier, too many public fund managers are judged by the standard of total return even though that measure is:

- At the bottom of the pecking order of investment policy mandates for safety, liquidity, and income, and
- A single-minded pursuit that diverts the attention every fund should pay to liquidity and safety.

As an alternative to total return, we advise funds to pursue a *market rate of return*, which we define as the 12-month moving average of 2-year U.S. Treasury note yields. Why did we pick this measure? There are three reasons:

1. It adapts well to the fiscal year budget cycle with which public fund managers must contend.
2. Unlike total return, a moving average of coupon yield smoothes out the extreme ups and downs caused by short-term market moves, producing a

more realistic snapshot of portfolio performance over the course of the budget cycle.

3. "The investment portfolio shall be designed with the objective of attaining a *market rate of return* throughout budgetary and economic cycles, taking into account the investment risk constraints and liquidity needs," according to the GFOA sample investment policy template.

To appreciate the difference between total return and a 12-month moving average of 2-year Treasury yields, consider Exhibit 3-3, which demonstrates the stability of this measure relative to the wild fluctuations (often including loss positions) of total return. In the figure, the top line is total return; it is the sum of the smooth coupon yield and the erratic bottom line, which is the portfolio's percentage value change due to a change in market value. Thus, the bottom line, total return equals return due to coupon plus return due to price changes. A fund manager can budget using the smoother yield line, but cannot possibly budget effectively when faced with the wild swings of the total return line. This explains more than anything else why total return is such an inappropriate measure of performance. The dominant workaday task of every fund is to produce stable cash flow and preserve principal. The fund manager who is forced to ride the bucking bronco of total return will accomplish neither.

Together, the five elements form the basis of a new, practical, and effective approach to measuring public fund performance. They remove measurement from the Temple of Total Return and assure that *all* three requirements of investment policy are addressed:

- Safety: through attention to interest rate risk and diversification
- Liquidity: by assuring that cash is available as needed
- Return: by tying return to a reasonable market rate of return

Even more important, they assure suitable portfolio choices.

Adoption of this new performance standard will effectively end current practices that compare fund performance to irrelevant market benchmarks, such as the Merrill Lynch 1–3 Year Government Index, and to the performance of other entities that have different requirements. It is a more

EXHIBIT 3-3
TWELVE-MONTH MOVING AVERAGE OF 2-YEAR TREASURY COUPON YIELDS
VERSUS TOTAL RETURN PERCENTAGE

MARKET RATE OF RETURN EVALUATION

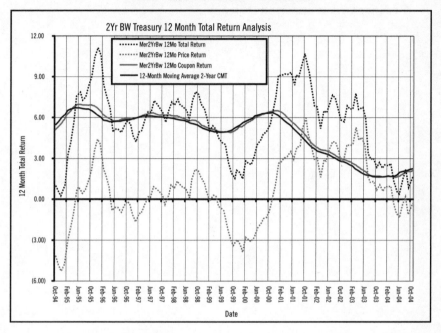

effective tool for evaluating the safety of principal for a public fund, and for determining whether a fund is providing adequate liquidity and an appropriate level of risk-adjusted return. The performance standard also serves as an early warning system, sounding the alarm if there is a problem in the making on any one of the three dimensions of fund performance: safety, liquidity, and return.

POINTS TO REMEMBER

- Total return is inappropriate as a measure of performance since it masks volatility and is not linked to what is suitable for a particular entity.
- Suitability is the one standard capable of specifying the performance measures appropriate to individual funds.

- Suitability has five aspects: liquidity, interest-rate risk, diversification, the legality of portfolio holdings, and appropriate market rate of return.
- It is recommended that managers adopt the 12-month moving average of whatever Treasury best reflects the fund's interest-rate risk as their standard for an appropriate market rate of return.

CHAPTER 4

Four Steps to Creating a Politically Correct Portfolio

Right price, Wrong bond.

—BEN FINKELSTEIN

KEY POINTS COVERED IN THIS CHAPTER

- Creating an investment plan
- Adopting a suitable management style
- Understanding risk
- Creating two virtual portfolios—one for liquidity, one for income

Previous chapters have described how investment policy creates a framework for what is legal in terms of the public fund. They have also dealt with the problem of doing what is both legal and suitable by means of an investment plan. Suitability, in our definition, addresses the safety and income requirements of a fund's stakeholders within the constraints of investment policy. This chapter takes the next logical step: it explains how fund managers can actualize their plans through the construction of *politically correct portfolios*—that is, portfolios that preserve principal while optimizing income at a level of risk that fund stakeholders are willing and able to accept. A politically correct portfolio is both legal and suitable, and this chapter offers a four-step process for creating one.

As you read this chapter, be cognizant of the endless tug-of-war between safety and income. Fund managers have a fiduciary responsibility to pursue both. In practice, most opt for safety since doing so satisfies a requirement set down in investment policy. In any case, safety represents the least political and career risk. For these safety-driven managers, the risk of loss is greater and more painful than the benefits derived from gains. A one-dollar gain, in their view, is not equal to a one-dollar loss. Thus, they will always favor loss avoidance over gain opportunities. Unfortunately, overadherence to safety leaves money on the table at the expense of the citizens to whom the fund manager owes a fiduciary responsibility.

As stated in chapter 1, virtually every fund is guided by an investment policy. Most are fairly standardized documents modeled on the Government Finance Officers Association, the Association of Public Treasurers of the United States and Canada, or some other source. These policies state the higher goals toward which fund managers should struggle, stipulate the constraints within which they should invest public money, and address issues of reporting and management. These are standard, static documents and do not recognize:

- The fluctuating and difficult-to-predict income needs of fund stakeholders. Fund managers must produce stable income for budget purposes
- Interest rate volatility
- Interest rate spreads among U.S. Treasury, agency, and corporate issues
- The need to monitor and justify investment decisions in relation to plan

Thus, fund managers need something more than an investment policy if they hope to play the game and win. We offer the following four-step solution:

1. Determine a suitable risk tolerance.
2. Define a management style.
3. Create an investment plan.
4. Construct a politically correct portfolio.

STEP 1: DETERMINE A SUITABLE RISK TOLERANCE

This step of portfolio construction has two components: determining the entity's *ability* to take risks, and determining its *willingness* to take risks. Ability and willingness to accept risk are two very different things.

Ability

The ability to take risks is largely economic and revolves around the following risk categories:

1. Liquidity risk: What percentage of the portfolio must be earmarked or dedicated to insuring that securities will not have to be sold prematurely to meet an obligation? The larger the liquidity requirement, the fewer dollars will be available for income investing.

2. Interest-rate risk: How much can the principal value of the portfolio fluctuate in response to interest rate changes in order to optimize income? This is largely a function of duration of portfolio assets. While the public fund investor intends not to sell securities to meet budget obligations, choosing the portfolio's interest-rate sensitivity is both a political and economic decision—political in that Governmental Accounting Standards Board Statement (GASB) 31 requires unrealized price changes on the portfolio to be reported, and economic in that decisions that attempt to reduce GASB 31 paper losses will most likely reduce the earning of the portfolio.

3. Credit risk: Should the fund invest in higher-yielding investment-grade issues or in default-free Treasuries? Many public funds whose state statutes allow investing in high-grade corporates choose to avoid or reduce the allocation to investment-grade debt. The motivation is mostly political. The shockwaves caused by Enron, WorldCom, and other debacles increased the political tensions surrounding investments in high-grade corporate bonds. Remember, a dollar loss carries much more weight in the minds of most public fund managers than does a dollar gain. While there is a very low probability of default for investment-grade corporate bonds with maturities of five years and less, the political anxiety of having to report a holding that is downgraded or might default is significant.

4. Reinvestment risk: Callable and mortgage-backed securities eventually force managers to reinvest principal at future, unknowable rates. For example, if a $100,000 bond is called by the issuer, you'll receive the final coupon payment and a return of your principal. But the chances are that you'll be faced with reinvesting at a lower rate, since the availability of lower rates are a principal reason for issuers to call their bonds.

Each of these risk categories has an impact on the portfolio's market value over time. We'll discuss the thorny issues they entail in the next chapter.

There are several ways of determining a fund's ability to take risks. The first is analogous to the situation faced by the individual investor. If Investor A has no immediate need for the interest, dividends, or periodic sales of securities in her portfolio, and she has plenty of financial resources, she can tolerate substantial portfolio risk, riding out down markets and the paper losses they cause. Investor B, in contrast, relies on a specified level of portfolio income to pay his bills each month. His risk tolerance is rock-bottom low; he cannot tolerate any price fluctuation on the down side. These very different individual investors have analogies in public funds, where some have large surpluses that allow them to invest more aggressively while others have limited surpluses and must follow a more conservative approach.

One way of determining an entity's risk-taking ability is to look back over the past few years and objectively determine its effectiveness in forecasting liquidity needs. An entity that has demonstrated little competence in this area will need a large margin of liquidity safety; otherwise it may be forced to sell bonds at the wrong time—when market value has dropped due to a rising in market interest rates. An entity that has demonstrated an ability to accurately forecast its liquidity requirements will require a lower liquidity level. Consider this example:

> Vernonville routinely provides its public funds manager with a forecast of the cash it will need during the coming fiscal year. This next year's forecast is for $1.5 million. Carla, being new to the job, has decided to do a little checking. She wants to know how reliable the city's forecasts have been over the past three years. What she finds is disturbing: the city's demands on the fund are never close to its forecasts, as shown below. Given the large variances from forecasts, Carla is not in a position to increase risks. She must tie up a substantial amount of funds in riskless, short-term, highly liquid assets. Otherwise she would run the risk of having to sell some assets prior to maturity—perhaps at losses.

Variances from Forecasts

Year	Forecasted Cash Need	Actual	Variance
2002	$ 900,000	$1,100,000	+22.2%
2003	1,000,000	1,400,000	+40.0%
2004	1,400,000	1,200,000	-14.3%

Yet another approach to estimating risk tolerance is to consider the size of the entity's budget surplus and/or rainy-day fund relative to expenditures. An entity with sufficient surplus cash is much more able to take risks than is one that has no such fund and no margin for error.

Willingness

Willingness is the other side of a public entity's approach to risk. Its willingness to take risks depends, in part, on the experience and investment expertise of the portfolio manager and/or supervisors. A fund manager who has been around the block more than a few times will usually be skilled in risk diversification and know when he is walking on thin ice and when he is not. He is a seasoned communicator, able to explain portfolio market value fluctuations in the context of the overall portfolio strengths and weaknesses.

The experience and sophistication of the fund's investment committee is another factor. Inexperienced committee members may be spooked whenever marked-to-market fund values show paper losses. If these members have their way, they will insist that most fund assets be invested in short-term, low-risk maturities. Their more experienced counterparts, however, will take market volatility in stride.

Most often, the willingness to take risks in balancing safety and income is essentially a political issue. Political risk deals with a trade-off between budget optimization and GASB 31 reporting—that is, between increasing fund income and the political risk of reported losses. Fund managers realize the catch-22 nature of their position: When rates rise and losses become recognized they are challenged by GASB 31; on the other hand, when they stay too conservative they are criticized (albeit probably not with the same zeal) for not producing more income.

Everyone in the public funds business understands these aspects of political risk, but few talk about them. The bottom line of this step is that the fund manager and the investment committee should reach an understanding about their willingness and ability to take risks as they address the perennial tug-of-war between safety of principal and income generation. That understanding will guide both portfolio construction and the actual selection of securities.

STEP 2: DEFINE A MANAGEMENT STYLE

The investment world has three types of inhabitants: traders, investors, and buy-and-hold participants. *Traders* represent the Wall Street Way and the pursuit of total return. Traders intend to sell securities before maturity and profit from price moves as the primary means of enhancing portfolio return. If they sense that the price of a security is about to rise, they establish a position and wait until they believe the moment is right to unload it and take a profit. If the security's price drops as anticipated, they may buy again.

Stock traders seldom evaluate the strategies of the companies they hold, long-term industry trends, or other "fundamentals" affecting these companies. Their focus is on the patterns of price and volume changes. "Everything you need to know about a company," say dedicated traders, "is in the tape"—that is, in the record of price and volume patterns. In the fixed-income market, the Wall Street trader seldom holds a bond to maturity. Instead, he follows an active strategy of harvesting profits when the time seems right and reinvesting in other opportunities. Wall Street money managers are not paid to be passive; they are paid to trade. There is a fine gap between trading and speculating in these cases.

Investors, in contrast to traders, look to the capital market risk premiums as the primary source for enhancing portfolio returns. They buy for the value they identify in a particular security—value not focused solely on market price. For the stock investor, that value is bound up in the future of the issuing company, a future that may be unrecognized by others, resulting in a low share price that will rise as other people catch on. For example, a person trained in fundamental analysis may find that XYZ Corporation's R&D pipeline is strong and predictive of much better future earnings than most people realize.

Value may be unrecognized for other reasons. For example, a company may have huge property assets that are not valued at market prices on the balance sheet; that value would be realized if the properties were sold or the company liquidated.

Value for the fixed-income investor is not derived from price change but from various risk premiums:

- The higher income offered by agency and corporate bonds over Treasuries of equal maturities (credit risk)
- The higher income available from callable and mortgage-backed securities (call and prepayment risk)
- The liquidity premium that investors can derive from bonds that may be difficult or costly to trade (market risk)
- Some combination of the above.

The public fund investor's quest for value goes hand in hand with the need to insure that forecasted budgets can be met without selling securities—just the opposite of the trader. **The public fund investor does not budget on the basis of hoped-for gains through price appreciation; that would be a recipe for disaster.** Through careful portfolio planning, the public fund investor assures herself that she will have the income to back up her budget—and doesn't count on uncertain paper gains to make it work. For the public fund investor, a stable budget dominates strategic moves. For traders, in contrast, market volatility rules, and dominates strategy. These managers look to coupons *and* price gains as their income sources. This is a risky business since no one can assure the price gains.

The investor may define his or her style in yet another dimension: passive versus buy-and-hold. The passive investor isn't like the trader, who buys and sells regularly in the hope that he'll pick up basis points here and there. Instead, this passive investor periodically rebalances his portfolio to bring it in line with budgetary necessities, the investment plan, changing risk factors, and a desire to have certain proportions of total portfolio value allocated to different maturities or bond qualities. Consider this example:

Sheila runs a $100 million fund for a large school district. Her investment plan is to have 25 percent of fund assets in 3- to 5-year U.S. Treasuries,

50 percent in 2- to 4-year U.S. Agencies, and the remaining 25 percent in highly liquid assets of 1-year or shorter maturities. All coupons and redemption payments are automatically swept into a money market account for later reinvestment.

If Sheila did nothing, time would upset her plan; everything owned by the fund would eventually mature and end up in the money market account. To avoid this, she must periodically rebalance her portfolio by reinvesting the money swept into the money market account. She may even have to do some judicious selling and buying.

Sheila is passive in the sense that she is sticking to a strategy of proportionality, making changes only to satisfy that strategy. This is much different from the buy-and-hold, set-it-and-forget-it style followed by many in the public funds field. Buy-and-hold has some important negatives. The first is the need for rebalancing just described; over time the fund will get out of balance and deviate from plan. The second negative is that it ignores portfolio strengths and weaknesses relative to prevailing market conditions. Finally, once security selections are made, the buy-and-hold portfolio manager adds no value in the sense of adjusting the portfolio to political and economic events and to income earning opportunities.

STEP 3: CREATE AN INVESTMENT PLAN

Chapter 2 described the reason for this important step. While policy is a rule book that applies generally to public fund managers, an investment plan is a playbook that recognizes the particular challenges of the individual fund and how it will satisfy the public entity's unique requirements for safety, liquidity, and income. The political process and year-to-year fiscal requirements should be accommodated in making an investment plan.

In a general sense, then, an investment plan is customized to the unique needs of the entity it serves. At the same time it provides a mechanism for monitoring the compliance of day-to-day portfolio tactics with the rules set down in the investment policy.

STEP 4: CONSTRUCT A POLITICALLY CORRECT PORTFOLIO

Step 4 is where the rubber meets the road. The previous steps are simply preparation. Constructing a politically correct portfolio should begin with the creation of two virtual portfolios: one for liquidity and another for income. This approach insures that the investment policy objectives of safety, liquidity, and income are properly prioritized.

Providing Liquidity: Two Portfolios

As stated earlier in this book, liquidity is a first-order concern. Inadequate liquidity means that a fund cannot meet its financial obligations without selling securities prior to maturity at the risk of principal loss.

It is recommended that the fund maintain a virtual liquidity portfolio within the total portfolio. That liquidity portfolio should be subdivided still further, into primary and secondary subportfolios, as shown in Exhibit 4-1 on the following page. The primary liquidity portfolio should contain maturities of 60 days or less. The purpose of this primary subportfolio is to assure that the fund will not be forced into prematurity sales. The actual securities in the primary basket should be cash-equivalents or assets convertible to cash at or near their cost basis. These would include U.S. Agency discount notes, short-term T-bills, commercial paper, banker's acceptances, state pools, and money market funds. The secondary liquidity subportfolio should contain assets with 61- to 360-day maturities. This secondary liquidity portfolio acts as a cushion against unexpected political or economic events that potentially require funds above the primary liquidity threshold. It fills an intermediate position for the fund, providing greater income than the zero- to 60-day assets, yet holding assets that are easily convertible to cash with a minimum of principal loss in the case of a fiscal emergency. These characteristics help the fund manager deal with the public fund dilemma of optimizing income while providing for both safety and liquidity.

In purchasing securities for these two liquidity portfolios, the manager should provide an adequate level of diversification. The fiasco of Orange County should be a warning to everyone that putting all liquid assets in one basket can turn a fund into a basket case. The protection gained through diversification can save the fund managers from big problems and headaches—including unemployment.

How Much Liquidity Is Enough?

Adequate liquidity provides a safeguard against the need to sell securities prematurely, potentially at a loss of principal. It makes security price volatility a nonissue and fulfills an important fiduciary responsibility of the fund manager. The question is, How much liquidity is necessary? This is an important question, because too much liquidity translates into less income.

Some people guess at their required level of liquidity (and we know some who guess very well); others simply use the previous year's figure. We suggest a more empirical method. One such method aims to determine both the most recent case and the worst-case scenarios for an entity's liquidity requirement. It begins by gathering the following key data:

1. The fund's lowest bank balance at the end of each of the last 36 months
2. The previous 36 months' disbursements (calculated monthly), excluding nonrecurring operational disbursements
3. Revenues received over the past 36 months (again, monthly), excluding nonrecurring revenue collections, large asset sales, etc.

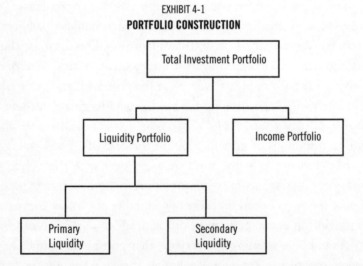

EXHIBIT 4-1
PORTFOLIO CONSTRUCTION

Once you have those data, you're ready for the first liquidity check. From your data select the following:

1. The largest monthly deficit (i.e., revenues less disbursement) during the past 12 months, and
2. The largest monthly deficit during the past 36 months.

Assuming no important changes in liquidity demands, these deficits indicate normal and expected liquidity parameters for which the fund must prepare. But what if events conspired to hit the fund with adversity on all three fronts at once? What if the fund experienced its lowest bank balance, its lowest revenues, and its highest expenditures in the *same* month—the worst-case scenario? To measure that worst-case scenario, use the following data:

1. The lowest fund bank balance over the previous 12 months
2. The largest disbursement over the previous 12-months
3. The lowest revenues collected in the last 12 months.

Once you have these data, make the following calculation:

       Lowest bank balance during the 12-month period
Plus   + Lowest revenue collected in any single month of the past 12
Less   − Highest disbursements total in any single month of the past 12

Equals = Worst-case liquidity scenario for the past 12-month period

Now do the same calculation using figures from the past 36 months.

These worst-case figures are every fund manager's "perfect storm" nightmare, bringing together the lowest standing bank balance with the worst revenue month and the highest disbursement month. How likely is it that these three storms will converge on your fund during the course of a single budget year? Not very likely. Nevertheless, a perfect-storm scenario should be the starting point for figuring how much should be available in the primary liquidity subportfolio, and how much in the secondary subportfolio. By identifying normal and perfect-storm surplus/deficit liquidity levels, the manager can tweak their actual investment portfolio's liquidity to the desired cash management cushion. Investment committee members should be engaged in this effort.

An alternative to the perfect storm method is to look back over recent years to identify variances from annual budget forecasts, as demonstrated in the box on page 39. If the highest variance from forecast is 40 percent, as shown in the example, that could be taken as the worst-case scenario and a guide to thinking and discussion of current fund liquidity.

What is the benefit of quantitative methods like these in determining the appropriate liquidity level of the portfolio? Simply put, they provide a basis for discussion and, if necessary, a defense in the case of future, unanticipated problems.

Seeking Income

Once the percentage of assets represented by the dollar amounts set aside for liquidity has been determined, the rest is available for the pursuit of income, as shown in Exhibit 4-2 for a $100 million total portfolio. The income portfolio seeks to optimize income within investment policy risk constraints. By optimizing income, the fund manager as a steward of public assets contributes to the well-being of the public entity and to the citizens it serves, be it a city, county, school district, or whatever. Optimizing income is a noble goal, and a reason for public fund managers to take pride in what they do, even though most citizens may be clueless about the manager's stewardship role.

Optimizing income within the bounds of prudence requires a keen understanding of both economic and political risks. It also requires some

EXHIBIT 4-2
ASSETS AVAILABLE FOR INCOME OPTIMIZATION

Total Portfolio Assets		100%	$100 million
−Liquidity Portfolio			
Primary	20%		
Secondary	10%		
		−30%	−30 million
=Income Portfolio		=70%	=$70 million

common sense in dealing with the reporting requirements of GASB 31, key topics we'll address in the next chapter.

Another aspect of income portfolio construction concerns the manager's approach to actualizing the investment plan through the purchase of securities. But before we get into that, consider the following tale:

Fred wants to build a summer home near the seashore but hasn't yet settled on the details of size, the style, the floor plan, or the finishing details. Nevertheless, Fred cannot resist a good deal when he sees it. The local lumberyard has a big sale on two-by-eight boards, so Fred buys a pick-up load of them. "These were a bargain. I'm sure that I'll find a way of using these boards," he tells himself. The next weekend the local Home Depot store reduces its price on roofing materials. Always eager to save money, Fred buys a pallet load of shingles and stores them in his garage. Before long, Fred's garage is filled to the rafters with assorted building supplies, bathroom fixtures, wiring, and kitchen appliances.

Eventually, Fred will build his seashore house, and he'll probably find a way to use all the items he has acquired piecemeal. Unfortunately, the characteristics of that house will be dictated by the materials stored in Fred's garage, not by the ideal plan that he and his architect should have drawn up and rendered into blueprints.

Some public fund managers behave like Fred. They forget that they are *portfolio* managers, not buyers and managers of individual securities. Their portfolios, in effect, are afterthoughts to opportunistic purchases. Instead of selecting securities that fit their plans, they buy securities pitched to them by various broker/dealers, each considered on its individual merits. The manager sees a block of agency bonds priced attractively and makes a buy. Two days later a local banker calls to tell him about some newly issued agency bond. Again, he makes a purchase. Before long, he has a collection of securities—every one of them legal, as defined by the investment policy—but not a portfolio that reflects his investment plan, his budget requirements, or the goals of fund stakeholders. Don't make this mistake. Always begin with an investment plan and purchase securities with the total plan in mind.

Managers should look at individual securities from a total portfolio perspective, asking, "How will this security fit my plan? How will it contribute to the risk and return profile of my portfolio?" This is what portfolio management is all about—to do otherwise would be security management. In effect, the manager should look at the portfolio as *one bond*. It is not ten separate $1 million securities, but a $10 million bond with a weighted average coupon of C, with a weighted average duration/maturity of D, with a weighted average purchase price of P, to yield a weighted average yield of Y. The securities purchased should complement this total portfolio, which means there are times to buy certain securities that are counterintuitive to typical practice. Consider these two examples:

Buying a security that fits the plan but yields less than other available securities. Sometimes, a T-bill is needed to balance the plan. But when was the last time a broker called to suggest a U.S. Treasury bill? Why? For the most part, there is no money in this transaction for the broker. Unless requested by the client, the broker will do what's in his or her own interest.

Buying a five-year security that fits the plan at a time when interest rates are rising. Why would a public fund purchase a longer-term security in a rising rate environment? The reason is that a public fund must produce stable earnings through all market cycles without speculation or market timing. This means that the interest-rate risk is defined in advance of market changes. Barring issues not anticipated when the investment plan was developed, the security should be purchased with the total interest-rate risk of the portfolio in mind, not the risk of the individual security. For example, a manager who is concerned about the interest-rate risk of holding a 5-year bond should stop worrying about the risk of that single bond or short-term performance of a market index and focus instead on the risk of the total portfolio, which might have an average maturity of only nine months. Adding the 5-year bond to the portfolio might extend the portfolio maturity by only a month. A plausible reason for the purchase of a five-year bond in a rising rate environment is to maintain or stay within the range of interest rate targets defined by the investment plan.

Creating a politically correct portfolio, as described in this chapter, requires both self-examination and thoughtful planning. Defining a management style and the risks that fund stakeholders can live with is the same "know thyself" self-examination upon which every type of responsible investing program is based. Constructing a politically correct portfolio structure is the pinnacle of planning; it must satisfy competing needs for safety and income as well as policy requirements for being suitable and legal. Getting each of these right is a major accomplishment. The next task is to populate the portfolio with individual securities that make the whole more than a collection of random parts.

POINTS TO REMEMBER

- An investment plan should be customized to the unique needs of the entity it serves, and should provide a mechanism for monitoring the compliance of day-to-day portfolio strategy within the rules set down in the investment policy.
- *Traders* intend to sell securities before they mature, looking to price moves as the primary means of enhancing portfolio return. *Investors* look to the capital market risk premiums as the primary sources for enhancing portfolio return. Passive investors periodically rebalance their portfolios to bring them in line with budgetary necessities, the investment plan, changing risk factors, and a desire to have certain proportions of total portfolio value allocated to different maturities or bond qualities.
- Portfolio construction should recognize the entity's ability and willingness to take risks.
- The fund manager should create two virtual portfolios: one for liquidity and another for income. The two together provide an effective construct for preserving principal while simultaneously earning income.
- **Constructing a politically correct portfolio recognizes that day-to-day investment decisions will be derived from what is suitable at the portfolio level, not what is legal at the security level.**

CHAPTER 5

Optimizing Income and Minimizing Risk

As people grow older they often mistake being careful with being wise.

—ANONYMOUS

KEY POINTS COVERED IN THIS CHAPTER

- GASB 31 and the problem of unrealized losses
- Political principal and economic principal
- Why funds must avoid over-concentration in government investment pools
- A strategy for dealing with price fluctuations
- A politically smart approach to evaluating risk/return trade-offs

As described in the previous chapter, adequate liquidity must be the portfolio manager's first order of business. It is the fund's best assurance against loss of principal, and is accomplished by creating a liquidity portfolio managed for that sole purpose. Adequate liquidity defends against the most realistic of principal risks—being forced to sell bonds at a loss prior to maturity.

Having attended to safety through diversification, and liquidity risks through primary and secondary liquidity portfolios, the manager can turn to the next and final investment policy objective: optimizing the income produced by the remaining principal. Some managers give too little attention to this part of the job, figuring "As long as the fund produces some income and no losses, I've done my job." This is often a safe thing to do. It's difficult to name a public fund manager sacked for earning too little as long as principal remained intact. As we've said, on Main Street, the political imperative to preserve principal exceeds the manager's motivation to increase income. Nevertheless, the fund manager has a fiduciary obligation to produce an appropriate and reasonable return for taxpayers. The following newspaper editorial excerpted from the *Las Vegas Review-Journal* is an example of the flack that some fund managers catch when they play it too safe.

> Do you know what the Clark County schools are doing with your money? Putting aside the persistent posturing for more and higher taxes, let's look at the other end of the equation: how much revenue the district generates from funds already on hand. Answer: Not nearly enough. With the state's third-largest investment portfolio, Clark County schools have some $600 million available at any given time. That's hardly petty cash. Heck, it would easily cover the support staff's bankrupt medical trust fund and any number of other bureaucratic boondoggles.
>
> The cache . . . has the potential to earn multimillion-dollar returns if invested competently.[1]

The editorialist goes on to state that the district's money managers are so conservative that they have earned very little revenue—far less than other government entities. While he admires their prudence, he notes that obsessive caution adds up, in his opinion, to a dereliction of duty on the part of the school district's money managers.

The writer aptly points out that a public fund has an obligation to do right by taxpayers by assuring that funds not earmarked for liquidity are invested prudently for income. Seeking income isn't simply a good idea; it is mandated by investment policy. But just as obsessive caution is wrongheaded, so too is an obsession with earning big returns, which is considered to have contributed to the fall of Orange County. Public fund managers should be obsessed with neither; their duty is to do what is prudent and suitable.

Investment income provides important benefits for constituents:

1. More public services and amenities. Citizens want parks, more teachers, firefighters, and new books for the library. In the end, there are only two ways

of paying for these public goods: taxes and portfolio earnings. When portfolio earnings are slim, citizens must either forgo these goods or pay higher taxes.

2. Reduced (or stabilized) taxes. This is every taxpayer's hope, and every elected politico's desire.

3. Funding of ongoing government operations. The costs of government payrolls, contracts, and supplies are high. Do you know any citizen who would complain about using fund earnings to help defray these costs? In the end, taxpayers must pay whatever bills their portfolio income fails to cover.

While the manager who focuses myopically on safety can say, "I did no harm," the manager who prudently optimizes income could minimize the need for a tax hike or a reduction in public services. The parks, new schoolbooks, and other public amenities made possible through portfolio income will be that manager's legacy to the community.

This chapter addresses the problem of producing income while minimizing risk. It does so through three fundamental questions: Should a public fund ever have a loss? What risk are we trying to minimize? and Why aren't all securities politically equal? The answers to these questions provide the fund manager with both conviction and clarity of purpose.

QUESTION 1: SHOULD A PUBLIC FUND EVER HAVE A LOSS?

The answer to this question is straightforward: Investment policy acknowledges that there may, in the course of business, be losses. It does *not* say "Take no risks." Instead, the language of policy encourages managers to identify and manage risks. This acknowledgment is a bitter pill for seasoned players in the public funds arena who know that risk, in career terms, is asymmetrical—that is, a dollar of gain is worth less than a dollar of loss. Wall Street operates with a different set of career rules. There, a portfolio manager can be fired for earning 5 percent when the index earns 6 percent; and can receive a fat bonus and a pat on the back for losing 5 percent when the index loses 6 percent. But not on Main Street, where realized principal losses can be career killers.

One source of potential loss is default by bond issuers. As described earlier, however, this risk can be minimized or mitigated for all practical purposes by investing in U.S. Treasury and U.S. Agency securities. Funds that invest in corporate bonds can also manage default risks by purchasing only high-quality issues and by diversifying among many issuers in different industries.

But the losses that concern us here are not the consequence of defaults. The ones that keep public fund managers awake at night are the unrealized losses that every bond investor experiences in a world of fluctuating interest rates. Anyone who invests in fixed-income securities understands that when prevailing market interest rates rise, the value of outstanding bonds drops—and the longer the term of the bonds, the greater the fall. This is the kind of loss that looks bad on paper but doesn't take a painful bite out of investment principal unless the manager is forced to sell. It is essential that managers—and their investment boards—understand this risk and differentiate between *recognized* and *realized* losses.

Recognized Versus Realized Losses

The term *recognized* is an accounting convention that refers to the mark-to-market value of a security or of an entire portfolio. Recognized profit or loss may be either realized or unrealized.

For public fund managers, a recognized but *un*realized loss does not mean that the issuer will fail to honor its coupon and redemption commitments; it means only that if the bond were sold, the recognized loss would be *realized*. For example, an investor who purchases a $1 million, 4 percent Treasury note at par may discover several months later that that same issue is trading at $950,000 due to an increase in market interest rates. From a strictly accounting perspective, she has recognized a $50,000 loss—an unrealized, paper loss. Other than that, nothing in her experience changes. She continues receiving the 4 percent coupons ($40,000 per year) and can look forward to receiving a redemption check for $1 million from the U.S. Treasury when the bond matures. If she were to sell that bond at $950,000, however, she would *realize* the loss. Realized losses and gains only result from the sale of a security.

Recognized but unrealized losses are not indications of poor performance or of something having gone amiss in the investment plan. The fund manager and investment advisory board should, in fact, expect occasional unrealized losses. We would go so far as to say that a portfolio that does not periodically have unrealized losses is a portfolio that is playing it too safe and not addressing its duty to optimize income! Unfortunately, the Governmental Accounting Standards Board (GASB) has complicated this straightforward approach to earning income for taxpayers through its Statement No. 31, which was issued in 1997 in response to the Orange County disaster of 1993 and to similar incidents in which public entities lost a great deal of money. GASB felt that the market value of securities held by governmental investment pools and other governmental entities (i.e., public funds) in those instances were not fully or properly reported to their constituents (mainly bondholders). As a remedy, they proposed that these pools and entities report investments at fair value on their balance sheets—"fair value" being the dollar amount at which a financial instrument could be exchanged in a current transaction between willing parties, other than in a forced or liquidation sale. Money market investments with less than one year to maturity would be reported under GASB 31 at *amortized cost,* or book value. Prior to the issuance of GASB 31, book value accounting was the preferred reporting for a portfolio.

In investigating Orange County, regulators found that governmental entities were reporting securities at their book value even though substantial losses would occur if they were liquidated. This practice of reporting at book value, and not disclosing the market value, overstated the financial health of entity in the eyes of municipal investors and the rating agencies. In the Orange County affair, reporting at book value instead of at market value was one reason that the problem was not discovered sooner—or allowed to occur at all.

The intent of GASB 31 was to provide better information to bondholders who are assessing the financial health of communities, states, and special districts that issue bonds to investors. Unfortunately, in their zeal to avoid a repeat of the Orange County disaster, the GASB accounting staff solved one problem by creating another. GASB 31 aimed to provide more complete disclosure to bond purchasers. However, this measure has vexed fund management and budget process.

GASB 31 required that "all investment income, including *changes in the fair value* of investments, should be reported as revenue in the operating statement" (italics added).[2] This change, which the regulators insisted would be of minimum impact to public funds, has confounded the budget process of public entities, shackling it to market volatility. As described by Kent Rock in his review of a preliminary draft of this book's manuscript, "GASB 31 was neither sensible nor a success. It succeeded only in misrepresenting and adding unnecessary volatility to financial reports." GASB 31 reflects what would happen if a manager sold his entire portfolio in one stroke, something that has probably never happened. Indeed, even the Orange County fiasco did not result in a complete sell-off.

Worse, GASB 31 has encouraged many managers to stay unnecessarily in short-term investment at the expense of public income. At a time when cash-strapped public entities should be realizing greater income from their funds, GASB 31 is punishing many who take that responsibility seriously. Fearful of showing paper losses, politically sensitive fund managers chose securities with maturities of less than 12 months! For taxpayers, this flight from possible paper losses has been costly because it has reduced the income returns of their funds.

Recognized but unrealized gains and/or losses can be problematic for a public fund from several viewpoints:

1. Inexperienced politicians may interpret paper gains as windfall money they can spend.
2. Paper losses cause politicians to hyperventilate and create a sense that things are not going as planned. Critics of incumbent office-holders use paper losses as evidence of incompetence.
3. Fund performance measurement can be misinterpreted.

To appreciate this last point, consider the public fund with the same 4 percent, $1 million Treasury note described earlier. Because of GASB 31, the fund manager will look like a loser, having gained $40,000 (4 percent) in income over the course of a year, but losing $50,000 (5 percent) due to an unrealized loss.

Income	$40,000
Marked-to-market loss	50,000
Annual performance	$(10,000)

The manager may be blamed for an overall 1 percent loss for the year. In this sense, GASB 31 sacrifices relevance for reporting form. Worse, as stated earlier, it encourages fund managers to own securities with maturities of less than one year; doing so insulates them from political heat should market prices fall, even though they earn very little on their funds.

Getting Past GASB 31

Granted, many seasoned professionals are no longer intimidated by GASB 31. They know that paper losses are inconsequential in the long run, and have educated their stakeholders to that point of view. But for every one of these, many other managers are afraid to do anything that isn't 12 months or less. And the millions they leave on the table must be made up through taxes and or reductions in public services.

So, how does a conscientious portfolio manager who seriously aims to optimize income within the bounds of prudent risk-taking operate in the world of GASB 31? The answer is education and communication. Consider this hypothetical situation, in which a treasurer explains fund performance to the finance committee of a city council.

"Ladies and gentlemen," she begins. "I thank you for this opportunity to report this quarter's fund performance. As you can see from my report, the fund has produced $274,000 in income during the third quarter, as forecasted. This amount represents bond coupon payments and interest earned on short-term Treasury and U.S. Agency securities and on our investments in the state pool. It does not include redemptions from maturing securities, nor any capital gains from prematurity sales, of which there were none this quarter."

One of the Councilors, a new member, has a question. "How is it that you are reporting a $274,000 gain when the statements in our packet show a decrease in the value of the fund of some $18,000?"

"That's a very fair question, Councilor, and I'm glad you asked it, since it goes to the heart of a common source of confusion about the performance of this and other public funds. The $274,000 I've just reported for the quarter represents real income that we've committed to City programs through the budget. The fund is budgeted to produce

$1 million for the City for the fiscal year, and, through the third quarter, we are squarely on track toward our goal.

"The loss you refer to, on the other hand, is the paper loss we would have incurred *if* we had sold all the securities in our portfolio at the then market value—which we did not. The Governmental Accounting Standards Board requires us to recognize the market value of our securities in our reporting, whether we sell them or not. Those values fluctuate day to day in response to market interest rates over which we have no control. Some days we're up, and some days we're down. But since we're not selling, it doesn't affect our ability to provide the income we've been budgeted to produce for the City—nor do these fluctuations produce *real* losses of principal."

At this point, the Treasurer hands each member of the committee a printed graph [similar to the one shown in Exhibit 3-3 in the text]. "The dotted top line of this graph," she explains, "represents the total return of the fund between June 30, 2004 and June 30, 2005. By total return, I mean interest and coupon payments *plus* any increases and decreases in fund value due to the day-to-day fluctuations just mentioned. As you can see, total return fluctuates erratically. The smoother, heavy line just below it is our fund's actual income, which is much more stable and predictable.

"If we were traders, we'd be following that jagged top line. Up one month, down another. But we're not traders. Except for occasional portfolio rebalancing, we don't trade. We invest in securities, harvest interest and coupons for the benefit of the City, and reinvest the principal when our securities mature. This is a prudent and proven way to manage public funds, and the *only* way whereby we can reliably produce the cash the City expects from us in the budget. Can you imagine the chaos that would follow if fund earnings were as erratic and unpredictable as the dotted top line of that graph?"

"I see what you mean," the Councilor responds, "but aren't you concerned about that top line?"

"I am concerned about the line insofar as it indicates a general trend in market rates," the Treasurer responds. "If I were a Wall Street bond fund manager I'd watch it like a hawk because my entire purpose would be to maximize total return. But total return is not the mission spelled out in the investment policy that guides our fund. Instead, our mission is three-fold: assure safety of principal, provide sufficient liquidity to meet financial obligations, and—only when those first two requirements are assured—optimize income for the City within risk parameters spelled out in the investment policy. And we have satisfied all three parts of our mission—despite the ups and downs of that total return graph, and despite having to report an occasional paper loss."

"I appreciate your comments about volatile total return," responds the Councilor, "but I'm still not clear on why we shouldn't be concerned about the reported losses in the market value of your portfolio securities. Doesn't this mean that we've lost some of our principal?"

"That's certainly an important question to ask," says the Treasurer, "so let me see if I can clear that up." At this point she hands out another graphic (Figure 1, opposite). "This graph indicates how rising interest rates can impact the market value of a $10 million portfolio of 2-year Treasuries. The top line indicates what happens when rates rise by 100 basis points, that is, 1 percent; the middle line indicates the impact of a 200 basis-point rate increase; and the bottom line presents the drop in reported value caused by a 300 basis-point increase. In the last case, the total market value of the fund drops by 6 percent. No fund manager would like to report this piece of news. Certainly not the trader, for whom recognized losses are *real* losses of principal. But for us, these losses are strictly theoretical—they are *unrealized.* And, as the graph indicates, unrealized losses disappear as time passes and the Treasuries move closer to maturity. If a fund manager simply waits until the maturity date, as we plan to do, the fund receives the full redemption value of its 2-year Treasuries. Not a dime of principal is lost!

"The long and short of this demonstration is that you shouldn't lose sleep over market-driven fluctuations in principal value. We could avoid them by investing entirely in short-term and money market securities. But if we did that we wouldn't be earning the $1 million you expect from us this year, and we would be failing on one of our three objectives: optimizing income. Instead of producing $1 million for the City budget, we'd be delivering $300,000 or less—and some services would need to be cut."

In this scenario, the treasurer has effectively articulated why GASB 31-reported fund performance should be ignored and enhanced income

FIGURE 1
RECOGNIZED LOSSES DISAPPEAR

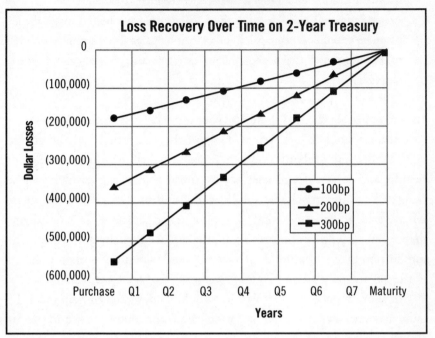

delivery emphasized. Fund income is within the control of the manager, and that control makes optimal budgeting feasible. GASB 31 results, in contrast, are beyond the manager's control and, therefore, are not a basis for budgeting. Once fund stakeholders understand this fact, the problem posed by GASB 31 goes away, and fund managers can concentrate on prudently optimizing income.

QUESTION 2: WHAT RISK ARE WE TRYING TO MINIMIZE?

Before trying to build and manage a politically correct portfolio to optimize income, we need some consensus about just what risk our investment policy is instructing us to minimize. The answer has important political and strategic implications for the investment decision process. The simple answer is that we should minimize principal risk. But let's be more specific about what we mean by "principal." As we use the term, there are two forms of principal: political and economic:

- *Political principal* is the dollar sum you invested today to produce income. It is also the dollar amount that remains after the income is spent.
- *Economic principal,* in contrast, is the actual income produced through the investment of political principal. Economic principal is also the sum committed to the budget and used to reduce administrative cost, pay obligations, or pay for public services.

Risk to political principal should be your foremost concern.

Readers surely recall Aesop's fable of the goose that laid the golden eggs. Well, think of that goose as political principal. As long as it remains healthy and intact, it will keep laying those golden eggs, which can be budgeted to support schools, public works, and so forth. It is unfortunate whenever a golden egg—that is, economic principal—is lost or squandered. But as long as the goose is protected, we can always recover. The implication here is that fund managers should take prudent risks in terms of the income they produce, but *safeguard political principal at all costs.*

In short, a public fund portfolio should be designed to help meet the budget requirements (economic principal) while giving protection to its ability to earn future income (political principal). There is no obligation to grow the egg-laying goose; to do so would require holding back some portfolio income for reinvestment, something that few cash-starved public entities would expect their fund managers to do. Simply protecting the goose is sufficient.

Before we drill further down to how a politically correct portfolio optimizes income, let's review. First, we recognize that in optimizing income some unrealized losses are inevitable; without them we could not generate the earnings mandated by investment policy. Second, the risk to be minimized is principal risk: specifically, the risk to political principal. Now we turn to the investment decision process of optimizing income. What do we buy and why?

QUESTION 3: ARE ALL SECURITIES CREATED EQUAL?

Chapter 2 made clear that not all investment policy objectives are equal in importance. The same can be said for securities; some possess risk characteristics that make them more politically correct than others. In the parlance of public fund investing, political correctness means putting political principal ahead of economic principal. Proper security selection helps us ensure that our goose remains as safe as prudently possible while keeping up it egg-producing activities.

So what risks should we be willing to assume? The financial world has many risks, ranging from geopolitical to counterparty risk, and from currency to inflation risk. Nevertheless, five financial risks dominate the world of public funds: liquidity risk, lack of diversification, credit risk, interest-rate risk, and reinvestment risk. We discussed liquidity risk in chapter 4. We'll deal with the others here.

Lack of Diversification

Lack of diversification is the Baby Face Nelson of this dangerous group. It looks innocent but can be extremely deadly, and usually takes the form of overconcentration in state and county investment pools (government investment pools, or GIPs). Many public funds use state and county pools as parking places for their liquid assets and idle short-term cash. This tactic may not be sound if a fund's liquidity assets are invested *solely* in these pools.

There is a great temptation to overconcentrate assets in GIPs, since these pools have most of the characteristics and conveniences of money market funds—but with higher rates. California's Local Agency Investment Fund (LAIF) is a prime example. LAIF consistently pays higher than normal money market rates, provides immediate liquidity, and has a $1.00 NAV (net asset value, which doesn't change) that makes it extremely attractive to fund managers. It also provides some internal diversification that small public funds might not be able to obtain on their own. LAIF functions like a typical money market fund, which we refer to as a "$1.00 NAV" fund because the net asset value remains constant at $1 per share. This has the benefit of offering price stability, even during periods of interest-rate fluctuations. But GIPs are *not* money market funds. They walk like a money market duck (stable 1.00 NAV), and they talk like one, too (daily access to funds depending on type of pool), but they don't have the same quack.

For starters, very few GIPs are rated. Next, some of the attractive and popular GIPs would fail the quality test of just about every investment policy. Consider LAIF. By Standard & Poor's rating system, LAIF would likely be rated below BBB, because its weighted average maturity is frequently 150 days, far beyond the 60 days required for a traditional AAA-rated money market fund. Second, these pools are not exempt from mark-to-market GASB 31 reporting requirements. Unless it qualifies as a "2a-7-like" fund, investments in a pool must be marked to market. Finally, GIPs usually hold longer maturities than do money market funds, and some of the securities they hold (such as corporate securities, mortgage-backed securities, repo transactions, etc.) may be forbidden by the investment policies of the public funds that put money into these same pools. Strange, isn't it—a public fund that is forbidden by policy from investing in corporate bonds is allowed, if not encouraged, to put its money into a government pool that invests in these unauthorized securities? Yet it happens.

The creditworthiness of these GIPs is in a sense based on the assumptions that they are (1) "too big to fail," and (2) the state would have a moral responsibility to make good on any losses. People assume that since pools are run by governments, governments will step in to prevent disaster. Unfortunately, there is no assurance, written or otherwise, that this will happen.

This is not to say that LAIF and other state and country pools are not excellent resources for public funds. GIPs are, in fact, practical substitutes for money market funds as primary or secondary liquidity investments. The problem, and the danger, is that fund managers are lulled into believing that GIPs are riskless. This is the classic free-lunch self-deception that leads many public funds to invest all their liquidity assets—and in a few cases their entire portfolios—in LAIF or other government pools. Concentrations like these are contrary to everything that experience teaches us about the need to diversify. Granted, few politicians will criticize a manager for placing a large percentage of fund assets in a GIP, particularly when those funds use the 3-month Treasury bill as their benchmark. On this basis, the fund and the politicians look good. The moral obligation assumption gives them further encouragement. Many invested heavily in the Orange County, California, pool with that same assumption and misplaced confidence.

One risk to these pools is the possibility that everyone will want to withdraw their money at the same time. If that happened, the pools would be unable to sell assets fast enough to pay investors, and they would surely have to sell some assets at losses. Thus, investors would have to wait for their money and possibly lose some of it unless government stepped in to make up the losses or, as many did in Orange County, either wait for a change in the market to restore their value or until the securities matured. The problem with these solutions is investors cannot wait for these corrective events to occur—public fund investments in GIPs are typically earmarked for operational liquidity. As John Maynard Keynes warned decades ago, "The market can stay irrational longer than you can stay solvent."

Granted, the risk of a run on GIPs is small and GIPs appear safe. But experience cautions us that "things happen," and the worst things that happen are usually the ones even smart people have failed to foresee. For evidence of this one needed only recall the collapse of Long Term Capital, a hedge fund whose board included two Nobel Prize–winning academics. The unforeseen default by Russia on its sovereign debt led to a near collapse in the financial markets. So the best advice is to diversify. Though GIPs appear safe and fund managers are encouraged to use them, a diversified allocation of fund assets is safer still.

One might argue that GIPs are diversified in the assets they hold, but they still represent a single basket to the public funds that participate in them. Common sense tells us not to put all of our eggs in one basket. State and county pools should be merely one of several "money market" or cash alternative investments for the liquidity portfolio of a public fund. Attempts to earn income without diversifying beyond a single pool, money market fund, or bank is dangerous and imprudent.

Credit Risk

Credit, or default, risk is another risk category with which fund managers must grapple in creating politically correct portfolios. *Credit risk* refers to a bond issuer's ability or inability to make timely interest payments and/or to repay the face value of its bonds at maturity. Anyone who follows the business news occasionally hears of a corporate debt issuer that has defaulted on its contractual obligations to bondholders. This is a newsworthy event when it happens—in large part because defaults are infrequent. More often, the corporate issuer's credit rating is reduced when its ability to pay falls into question—from AAA to AA, from AA to A, or from A to BBB. Rating reductions in and of themselves do not jeopardize the ability to pay interest and repay principal at maturity. They do, however, indicate a greater risk of default and, as a consequence, lower the market value of the affected bonds. In practice, a rating downgrade has a political cost.

Despite the credit risks, public funds that are allowed to invest in corporate debt can usually capture a higher return from corporate bonds than from equal investments in default-free government debt. They can manage the greater credit risks through diversification and/or by purchasing issues with A or better credit ratings. Many public funds, however, are prohibited from purchasing corporate issues. Indeed, these funds generally confine portfolio purchases to:

- U.S. Treasury bills, notes, and bonds, which are viewed as having no credit risk because they are backed by the full faith and credit of the United States government
- Federal government agency debt issues (agencies), which are backed either de jure or de facto by the federal government

In their zeal to be absolutely safe, some managers steer clear of agencies, forgoing the higher interest income they offer. This is unfortunate since the credit risk in agencies is AAA and carries the implicit backing of the U.S. Government. Can you recall the last time a federal agency issue

---

A CAVEAT ABOUT PUBLISHED CREDIT RATINGS

In sizing up risk, investors look to debt issue credit ratings published by Standard & Poor's, Moody's, Duff & Phelps, and Fitch. Their Aaa (AAA), Aa (AA), and lower ratings of creditworthiness are useful guides. These ratings, however, are not foolproof indicators of default risk. Because rating companies cover so many issues, they can only review each issue periodically. And bad things can happen between those reviews. Thus, we have some well-chronicled fiascos such as the default of two issues of Washington Public Power Supply System bonds in the early 1980s; these went from the highest ratings to default in a blink of the eye. Diversification is the best antidote for these possibilities.

defaulted on its obligations? The default risk in agencies, while remote, generally provides passive investors an excellent risk/return trade-off relative to U.S. Treasuries. Thus, by prudently adding some agencies to the portfolio, a manager can pick up additional income with minimum additional credit risk.

Interest-Rate Risk

Interest-rate risk refers to the market price volatility that fixed-income securities experience as a consequence of changing market interest rates. As every experienced investor knows, the market value of a previously issued bond rises when market interest rates decline, and does just the opposite when rates rise. A fund holding fixed-income securities is always exposed to this type of risk.

The impact of interest-rate change on the mark-to-market value of a fixed-income security is a function of three things, assuming that other factors, such as creditworthiness, remain the same: the magnitude of the change, the time to maturity of the security, and the size of coupon payments. It's intuitively obvious that a big swing in market rates—say, 2 percent—will

---

RULES TO REMEMBER

For the inexperienced public fund manager or investment board member, here are some general rules to remember with respect to interest rate risk:

- Bond values drop when market interest rates increase, all other factors being unchanged.
- Bond values increase when market interest rates decrease, all other factors being unchanged.
- Long-term bond values are more heavily impacted by interest-rate swings than are short-term bonds, all other factors being unchanged.
- Zero-coupon bonds and bonds purchased at discounts to redemption value are more heavily affected by market interest swings, all other factors being equal. This is because so much of their benefit to the investor comes at maturity—100 percent of it in the case of zeros. (We will explain the details in chapter 8.)

affect a bond's market value to a greater degree than will a small swing—say, 0.25 percent. We saw clear evidence of that in the graph on page 59.

A Strategy for Dealing with Price Fluctuations

Price behaviors keep portfolio managers from capturing the higher income that comes from long-term securities. Fearful that their stakeholders will confuse recognized (i.e., mark to market) losses with realized losses, they stay short and accept lower income. In doing this they achieve the most pressing political goal of showing no loss of principal (realized or unrealized), but they fail on the economic front of providing greater income. What can be done to remedy this situation? One strategy for reducing the impact of market volatility on reported portfolio value—while gaining the benefit of high returns—is to substitute credit risk for interest-rate risk. Consider the following two portfolios:

Portfolio A	Portfolio B
U.S. Treasuries	U.S. Agency securities (noncallable)
No credit risk; higher interest-rate risk	Higher credit risk; lower interest-rate risk
Market value: $116,540,000	Market value $116,540,000
Portfolio yield: 5.51%	Portfolio yield: 5.56%
Portfolio maturity: 2.25 years	Portfolio maturity: 10 month
Portfolio duration*: 2.14	Portfolio duration: 0.84
DV01**: $24,777	DV01: $9,653

* Duration is the sensitivity of a bond's price expressed as the percentage change in price for a 100 basis point change in yield. It represents the weighted average present value of the bond's future cash flows where the present values serve as the present value weights. Higher duration translates into higher price volatility due to interest-rate changes. Note: Duration will be covered in chapter 8 of the book.

** DV01 is the dollar value change in portfolio value given a 1 *basis point* change (0.01%) in interest rates.

Notice in this example how the portfolio manager has obtained essentially the same yield with far less price volatility risk by switching from all Treasuries to all agencies of shorter maturities. In fact, the price volatility risk of Portfolio B is 61 percent less than that of Portfolio A. Thus, the manager has kept the same level of current income (trading reinvestment risk for price risk as well) while reducing the political risk of having to report an unrealized loss of principal.

What about the greater credit risk of Portfolio B? Yes, there is a greater credit risk with agencies, but, as stated above, the credit risk in agencies is comparatively conservative when contrasted to the increased interest rate risk of USTNs, *and* that risk can be reduced through diversification.

Reinvestment Risk

Many investors overlook *reinvestment risk*—the risk that they will have to reinvest coupon payments and redemptions at lower rates of return. If one must reinvest at lower rates of return, the portfolio return will decline. Consider this example:

> The Green Valley Water District fund owned a $1 million, 3-year, 4 per-cent Treasury note. This note produced $40,000 in annual coupon income for the district's budget. When the three-year period had run its course, the portfolio manager used the redemption proceeds to purchase another $1 million, 3-year Treasury, but now the going coupon rate was down to 3 percent. This reduced the district's annual income by $10,000.

The opposite could also occur: With rates on 5-year Treasury notes higher than 4 percent, the income will increase.

Like interest-rate risk, reinvestment risk is one of the hazards with which public fund managers must contend, and it poses a perennial strate-gic dilemma: Assuming that liquidity needs have been met, should the manager lock in a good rate for many years by purchasing 4- to 5-year bonds, and then face the problem of principal volatility due to interest rate swings? Or is it better to stay short? Staying short reduces principal volatility but produces less income at the same level of credit quality. Short-term investing also raises the spector of reinvesting at a lower rate in the future.

The reinvestment dilemma is complicated further when callable bonds are introduced, as in this example:

Deborah has cash to invest. As she sees it, the best opportunities are:

1. Five-year Treasury notes, available at par with a 5 percent coupon, and
2. Five-year callable agencies, also available at par with a 6 percent coupon. These newly issued agencies have two-year call protection.

Deborah wants as high a return as she can prudently obtain, but she's very nervous about her options. "If I buy the T-note," she tells herself, "I can hold onto that 5 percent yield for five years. If I buy the agency, there's a chance that it may be called away after two years. Who knows what rate I'll be able to reinvest in then."

If Deborah decides to buy the callable agencies, she will have increased her portfolio yield at less interest-rate risk. That is a worthy accomplishment. However, she will have increased the reinvestment risk. If market rates were to drop significantly, it's almost certain that the agencies would be called away from her at some point after the two-year call protection period expired, robbing her of a high rate and forcing her to reinvest at the prevailing lower rate. But this is only one possible scenario of three. The other two are:

*   Interest rates stay roughly the same. Deborah wins because her callable agencies are unlikely to be called. She keeps the higher interest rate for the full term of the bonds.
*   Interest rates rise. Deborah wins again because her callable agencies will definitely not be called. If they were called, she could reinvest the principal in bonds with even higher yields.

Chances are that you find yourself in Deborah's position all the time. You must look at apples-and-oranges choices and decide which choice is most prudent. The next time this happens, ask yourself these questions:

*   Which choice best balances the tug-of-war between safety and income?
*   Which represents the best income-versus-risk combination? Remember that if your liquidity needs are already covered by the liquidity portfolio, you can focus more on income and less on paper losses.

- Which choice is best for your budget? If you must optimize income, you take reinvestment risk over interest-rate risk.
- Which choice offers the greatest marketability (bid/offer spread)? Here, remember that Treasuries always enjoy greater marketability than agencies and corporates. Small issues of other securities are even harder to sell without paying higher transaction costs.

Reinvestment risk would not be a problem if we had foreknowledge of future interest rates. But accurate insights into future rates are hard to come by. "Our analysis of semiannual U.S. Treasury bond yield forecasts as presented in the *Wall Street Journal* shows that the consensus forecast is poor. Over the past 43 forecast periods, the consensus estimate of the yield change has been wrong in direction 65 percent of the time."[3] In the short term (one year or less), economists can usually forecast the *direction* of future rates, though their estimates of the degree of rate changes vary from one economist to another. Beyond one year, you'd do just as well to consult your barber; his guess about future interest rates is probably as good as that of any Wall Street economist. Neither can give you a reliable forecast beyond a year or two.

MAKING TRADE-OFFS IN A POLITICAL WORLD

With our discussion of diversification and risk now complete, let's move on to the political implications of certain tradeoffs—implications that money managers on Wall Street see as strictly economic issues. Optimizing income within the bounds of prudence forces Main Street managers to make trade-offs between the safety of political principal and budget income (or economic principal). In some cases these trade-offs are made solely for political reasons; in other cases they are purely economic.

As an example of a purely political trade-off, consider a public fund that must sell a security prior to maturity in order to meet an unanticipated obligation. (This is not to be confused with a public fund freely choosing to rebalance its portfolio, a topic we will address later.) In this case, Security A is a $1 million Treasury note purchased at par (100), which now has a market value of 95, or $950,000. Its coupon is 4 percent. A sale at this point would mean a permanent loss of $50,000 in political principal. The budget assumed 4 percent on a million or $40,000 a year. If the sale were made, the fund would lose $50,000 in principal and $40,000 more in income earmarked for the budget.

Security B is a U.S. Agency note, likewise bought at par (100), which now has a market value of 99. Its coupon is 5 percent. Sale of this note would mean a permanent principal loss of $10,000—substantially less than the Treasury loss of $50,000.

Using our definitions of political principal (original investment) and economic principal (income), and remembering that stewardship mandates the safeguard of political principal above all else, then the politically correct decision would be to sell the higher yielding agency and keep the lower yielding Treasury. Here you have a classic political decision driving economics.

Wall Street would view this trade as economically unsound. It would advocate selling the lower yielding, lower transaction cost, more liquid Treasury. On Main Street, however, the portfolio manager would be hard-pressed to explain the logic of losing $50,000 in principal when he had the option of losing only $10,000. When buying securities, circumstances like this one must be anticipated and included in portfolio construction and strategy.

As an exercise in making trade-offs, consider Exhibit 5-1, which asks you to rank the capital market risk of securities in political terms. By "political terms" we mean factoring the worst outcome for one's career and a politician's reelection effort into one's investment strategy. As you do this exercise, recall that we have two dominant goals: preserve political principal (the original investment), and optimize income for this year's budget. Growth has little role in fund strategy. In ranking the political risks, ask yourself which exerts the greatest influence on public and political perceptions.

EXHIBIT 5-1
RANK THE POLITICAL RISKS

Credit risk	_____ %
Interest-rate risk	_____ %
Reinvestment risk	_____ %
Total	100 %

Are you curious about how other public fund managers and board members rank these risks? Exhibit 5-2 is a representation of how participants in our seminars over the past ten years have, on average, ranked the three risks. As you can see, interest-rate risk leads the pack, and by a huge margin. This is undoubtedly prompted by the impact of GASB 31 on financial reporting, and by the very real danger of losing political principal if and when securities must be sold prior to maturity. It also reflects how people rank the risk versus return trade-offs they face in optimizing portfolio income.

EXHIBIT 5-2
AND THE RESULTS ARE . . .

Credit risk	20%
Interest-rate risk	70%
Reinvestment risk	10%
Total	100%

Interest-Rate Risk Versus Credit Risk

With risk type comparisons in mind, consider two securities, a USTN and a U.S. Agency, with the same yield. One has less credit risk but more interest-rate risk—the USTN; the other has less interest-rate risk but more credit risk—the U.S. Agency. Based on this information alone, which do you suppose is riskier? We would suggest that the first, the one with the greater interest-rate risk is more risky; perhaps 3.5 times more risky (70 percent is 3.5 times more risky in participant view than credit of 20 percent). The answer is determined by which poses the greater threat to political principal (the goose). Since a premature sale is far more likely than a default on either of the securities, interest-rate risk dominates.

Interest-Rate Risk Versus Reinvestment Risk

Now, let's shift gears and compare two more securities—a 5-year U.S. Agency bullet and a 5-year U.S. Agency callable—again with the same yield but differing in other respects. The first has more interest-rate risk and less reinvestment risk; the second is just the opposite, with less interest-rate risk but more reinvestment risk. Again, we think that the one with the higher interest-rate risk is the riskier of the two, and for the same reason: its potential to imperil political principal in the case of a premature sale is higher. Politically speaking, it may be seven times more risky than the security with less interest-rate risk but more reinvestment risk. Here again we have eggs-versus-goose situation. Reinvestment risk can cause a loss of eggs (future income) but with less risk to the goose (lower interest-rate risk). Interest-rate risk focuses on the eggs at the expense of the goose. And we should be more concerned with the egg producer than with the egg production. It is the goose, after all, that assures a stream of future income.

Credit Risk Versus Reinvestment Risk

Now let's try another risk combination, this time of two securities with equal yields—a single A medium-term corporate note and a triple A callable U.S. Agency: the first has more credit risk and less reinvestment risk; the second has less credit risk and more reinvestment risk. Which do you think poses the greater political risk to the fund? We would suggest that the first poses twice the political risk of the second. Why is that? We justify this conclusion on the fact that securities with credit risk, while having more stable income, carry greater risk of a downgrade or default, which would potentially cut into political principal—anathema for public fund managers. The other bond's major risk is the possibility that reinvestment may produce less income (economic principal), a secondary concern for the manager.

As this chapter has demonstrated, the public fund is obliged to optimize income. But it must do so with the safety of political principal as its first priority. When push comes to shove, the well-being of the egg-laying goose matters much more than the goose's eggs. The manager who kills or injures the goose will himself be a cooked goose.

POINTS TO REMEMBER

- A portfolio that does not periodically have unrealized losses is a portfolio that is likely playing it too safe and not addressing its duty to optimize income.
- GASB 31 requirement for marked-to-market investments has the effect of intimidating fund managers to overly short investments, reducing income to their stakeholders.
- Managers must educate stakeholders to the differences between realized and unrealized losses—and their consequences for fund performance.
- Political principal is the dollar sum you invested today to produce income. It must be safeguarded above all else.
- Economic principal is the income produced by earnings on the investment of political principal.
- Avoiding risk is not managing risk.
- Fund managers should avoid overconcentrations in government investment pools.
- Credit risk can be managed through diversification.
- In trading off one risk for another, managers should put priority on limiting political risks to principal.
- GASB 31 is a reporting requirement, not an investment strategy.
- Securities are not politically equal when it comes to protecting principal and optimizing income.

PART TWO
TECHNICAL TOOL KIT

CHAPTER 6

Opportunity Cost

Observe the opportunity.

—ECCLESIASTES

KEY POINTS COVERED IN THIS CHAPTER

- Optimal maturities for fund investments
- What suboptimal maturities are costing taxpayers
- How to calculate the opportunity costs of alternative securities
- Opportunity cost from the taxpayer's perspective

Many public fund managers follow a simple and intuitive approach to investing. They set aside whatever is needed for liquidity purposes and simply *ladder* the rest—that is, they invest all funds not required for liquidity in securities with progressively longer maturities. Their choice of maturities is determined less by what is optimal than by the rule book of permissible securities, and by what will shelter the manager from the risk of having to report any GASB 31 losses.

This chapter offers a different approach, one that will help you to accomplish three economically and politically vital tasks:

- Determining the optimal maturity for your portfolio. The optimal maturity, in most cases, will produce more income than you might expect. The methodology behind this task will help you answer the question, "Why did you select these particular maturities?"

- Quantifying the opportunity cost of holding maturities that are too short, owing to GASB 31 concerns. Going too short simply to avoid reported but unrealized losses carries a real cost that stakeholders often overlook. **If they knew that opportunity cost, their views on GASB 31 would likely change.**
- Calculating the amount of taxes that would have to be raised in order to produce the income forgone through the choice of maturities that are too short. If you want see your investment board members sit up and listen, just tell them how much they'll have to raise in taxes to make up for unduly short-term investments.

The techniques offered in this chapter will help you construct the optimal portfolio, give you a powerful method for explaining your security selections to key stakeholders, *and* help those stakeholders understand the cost to taxpayers of alternative choices.

THE RIGHT MATURITY

If insufficient liquidity is the primary risk to a portfolio, as described earlier, then interest-rate risk is the second. In fact, these risks are two faces of the same predator. Insufficient liquidity forces the fund manager to sell bonds prior to maturity—and at a loss if market interest rates have risen since the bonds were purchased. It is amazing how many public funds operate without a strategy for dealing effectively with interest-rate risk. In the worst cases their managers simply hide from it by staying short. The consequence, of course, is paltry income. In other cases, managers ignore interest-rate risk and put assets not reserved for liquidity into a "ladder" of bonds with different noncallable maturities—for example:

$200,000 in a 1-year agency bond
$200,000 in a 2-year agency bond
$200,000 in a 3-year Treasury bond

This has the appearance of a great strategy. Every year, a large chunk of the income-oriented portion of the portfolio will mature, allowing the manager to reinvest in another 3-year security at the prevailing rate. The strategy also captures short- and medium-term rates, hedging the risk of being too long or too short as market rates move. The overall maturity of the portfolio, then, is a function of the ladder and *not* an optimal relationship between yield and maturity.

But how can that optimal relationship be found? History provides a guide. Exhibit 6-1 contains Merrill Lynch data on risk/return trade-offs for the ten-year period ending October 31, 2004. Once you understand what its numbers represent, you will have a much better sense of which maturities offer the biggest bang (returns) for the investment buck (risks). One would assume that return and risk in an efficient financial market would move in lockstep. As the exhibit reveals, however, that assumption would be wrong. It is often possible to get a substantial portion of the potential reward with a less substantial increase in risk.

But first, some technical explanations. Risk for investors is a function of uncertainty and volatility, and is most often represented through *standard deviation*. Standard deviation is a widely used measure of risk. It refers to the tendency of returns to cluster around an average, and indicates the degree to which returns are dispersed around that average.

Thus, while we might say that the average 12-month total return of 2-year Treasuries (USTNs) over the ten-year period was 5.55 percent, that

EXHIBIT 6-1
BELLWETHER U.S. TREASURY TOTAL RETURN ANALYSIS, OCTOBER 31, 1994 TO OCTOBER 31, 2004

Index	Avg 1Yr Total Return	Standard Deviation	% of 30-Year Return	% of 30-Year Risk
3Mo Tbill	4.34	1.73	54.80%	15.99%
6Mo Tbill	4.58	1.75	57.83%	16.17%
2Yr Treasury	5.55	2.58	70.08%	23.84%
5Yr Treasury	6.63	5.07	83.71%	46.86%
10Yr Treasury	6.98	7.39	88.13%	68.30%
30Yr Treasury	7.92	10.82	100.00%	100.00%

Reprinted by permission. Copyright © 2005 Merrill Lynch, Pierce, Fenner & Smith Incorporated.

Note: In this exhibit, Average 1Yr Total Return is the average of every one-year total return of the benchmark security between 10/31/94–10/31/04. Standard Deviation is the standard deviation of the above one-year total returns.

single number conceals the fact that some returns were less and others greater than 5.55 percent during that ten-year span of time. Standard deviation gives us a sense of how closely returns on 2-year Treasuries clustered around the average during the ten-year period. The tighter the cluster around the average, the lower the standard deviation, and vice versa.

For a graphic depiction, look ahead to Exhibit 6-2, which shows two bell-shaped curves around the same average return. The curve with the range of outcomes closest to the average—Security A—has a lower standard deviation than Security B, whose outcomes range more broadly. For our purposes, just remember that a low standard deviation indicates that the return of an investment—based on historical data—is likely to fall fairly close to the expected return. Its outcome is less uncertain. A high standard deviation indicates that the actual return will fall somewhere in a wider range on either side of the expected return. The degree of uncertainty—that is, the risk—is higher.

Now that you understand risk and standard deviation, we can put the information in Exhibit 6-1 to work. Let's begin by comparing the returns and standard deviations of the 3-month and 30-year Treasuries—the opposite ends of the yield curve. As a fund manager, you want to get the highest return you can with the least amount of risk. The 3-month T-bill, as you would easily guess, returned substantially less—54.80 percent of the 30-year alternative. But the risk, as measured by standard deviation, was only 15.99 percent of the risk of the 30-year UST bond. This affirms the timeless logic that those who seek higher returns must take higher risks.

But what is the optimal trade-off between return and risk? Obviously, no public fund manager would purchase 30-year UST bonds with the intention of holding them to maturity, though every manager would love to capture their higher returns. But almost no one would want the risks associated with holding long-term bonds. The challenge, then, is to find a return that meets your income needs at a risk level that you and fund stakeholders can live with.

The data in Exhibit 6-1 quantify the risk/return trade-offs from which a real portfolio can be selected. We recommend analysis of the data as a tool for optimizing investment choices. To cite just one example, consider the 2-year USTN. It provides 70.08 percent of the 30-year UST bond's return with only 23.84 percent of the risk. That seems like a worthwhile trade-off. Indeed, most managers would gravitate toward this maturity. Furthermore, they can use the data—which are easily obtained and updated—to quantify and explain their portfolio choices to fund stakeholders and overseers. We know of no better way to do this.

RISK AND FUND PERFORMANCE

Our discussion of returns and standard deviation also underscores a point hinted at back in chapter 3, that return alone should not be the sole measure of fund performance; the volatility of returns should be part of performance appraisal. Exhibit 6-2 helps explain why.

EXHIBIT 6-2
TWO PORTFOLIOS

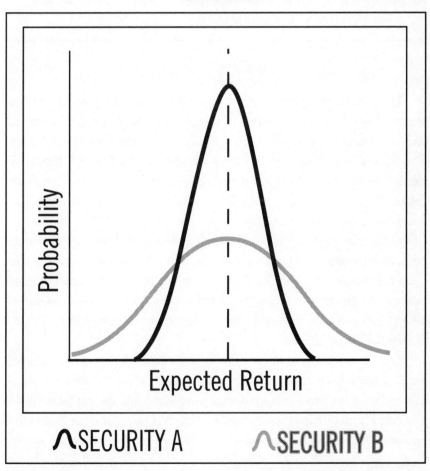

PUTTING STANDARD DEVIATION TO WORK

Standard deviation can help you estimate the probable outcomes of your security selections. Here's how: Statisticians have determined that approximately 95 percent of outcomes within a normal distribution will fall within plus or minus 2 standard deviations of the average. Let's apply this to the data we've shown in Exhibit 6-1. Looking at the 3-month average return of 4.34 percent, which has a standard deviation of 1.73 percent, we could say that 95 percent of one-year-period returns on the 3-month T-bill would fall between 0.88 percent (4.34 − 2 x 1.73) and 7.80 (4.34 + 2 x 1.73) percent. Even in the worse case, the return (0.88 percent), is still positive. If we apply this method to the 30-year bond, which has an average annualized total return of 7.92 percent and a standard deviation of 10.82 percent, then 95 percent of returns would likely fall within a wide band of −13.02 percent to +29.56 percent. That's quite a range, and a substantial loss of principal in any one-year holding period is possible.

Here we see two portfolios with the same expected return (the dashed vertical line), based on ten years of actual performance data. The vertical axis represents the probability that the expected return will be achieved. Portfolio A's expected return is exactly the same as Portfolio B's, but, as indicated by it curve, it has been more consistent in its annual performance. Thus, the returns of Portfolio A have been less volatile, and hence less risky. Its probability of having a terrible year is less.

Unfortunately, when elected officials are comparing average annual return, they frequently do so without considering performance volatility. To use a baseball analogy, they hire a player with an impressive batting average without regard to the consistency of that person's performance—something that would matter enormously if their new player went into a slump during the World Series.

Getting back to the world of fund investing, let's consider two hypothetical portfolio managers: Harry and Harriet. Over the past five years, Harry's fund has produced an average return of 5 percent per year. At 4.8 percent, Harriet's hasn't done quite as well. But now consider the returns shown in Exhibit 6-3. Here we see that Harry's returns have been all over the map. He's had some spectacular years and some truly dreadful ones. Harriet, in contrast, has been far more consistent. Which of these managers would you hire to handle your money?

EXHIBIT 6-3
ONE MANAGER PRODUCES MORE CONSISTENT RESULTS

| | Annual Returns | | | | | |
	2000	2001	2002	2003	2004	Average Return
Harry	7.0	6.0	2.0	8.0	2.0	5.0
Harriet	5.2	4.7	4.8	5.0	4.3	4.8

OPPORTUNITY COST

Having explained how a public fund can quantify their portfolio's optimal interest-rate risk versus return, let's move on to the consequences of not using this approach. More specifically, let's quantify the consequence of suboptimizing the risk/return profile out of fear of incurring unrealized losses à la GASB 31.

Many public funds insist on being short in the name of safety—both economic and political. Safety of either type, of course, produces an opportunity cost for taxpayers and for the direct fund stakeholders in the form of forgone income. *Opportunity cost* is a fundamental concept of economics. We define it as the value of an alternative not taken.

Once you understand this concept, you'll recognize it in many facets of your life and your job. Consider this example:

> Jane, a high-school senior, was urged to use her $150,000 trust fund to earn a college degree from an Ivy League school. "College grads earn roughly twice as much as high-school grads over their lifetimes," Jane's counselor told her.

The counselor in this story was factually correct. College graduates do earn significantly more money. But he failed to mention the opportunity costs of his suggested course of action, namely:

- the job earnings that Jane would give up during her four years of study
- the trust fund principal and interest that would gradually disappear—instead of growing—as she paid for her schooling

Over the long haul, going to college might produce an economic benefit for Jane, but the true measure of that benefit cannot be known without factoring her opportunity costs into the analysis.

Public fund managers likewise should consider the opportunity costs of their decisions, particularly when making trade-offs between safety and income, as in this example.

John's fund received a $100,000 interest return on its investment in U.S. Treasuries over the previous one-year period. Had John invested in U.S. Agencies over the same period instead, his return would have been $120,000. The difference—$20,000—represents the opportunity cost of his decision.

In the absence of other information, it's not possible to know if John made a wise choice. Calculating the opportunity costs, however, quantifies the economic cost of that choice. He forfeited $20,000 in order to obtain another benefit. That other benefit might be political, or it might be economic. Here are two possibilities:

- Two of John's investment board members fear the greater default risk of agencies: "We don't want to take any chances or expose ourselves to criticism if something were to go wrong." (Political).
- John's fund must stay as liquid as possible because the water district served by the fund is never sure how much cash it will need during the year. Treasuries can be sold more readily than agencies and with less loss of principal. (Economic).

The question for John and his board members is simply this: Is either of these benefits greater than the $20,000 opportunity cost they impose on the fund? John could use this information to educate his board members about the cost their fear of U.S. Agencies imposes on fund performance. Likewise he could show his fund officials how their failure to give him a reliable projection of cash needs is costing the fund $20,000 each year. Opportunity cost, then, puts the ball in the court of the officials, forcing them to take responsibility for the decisions that so often suboptimize portfolio income.

Now that you understand opportunity cost, recall in chapter 4 the discussion of a public fund's ability and willingness to take risk. Let's revisit the data in Exhibit 6-1 to see how it would impact the fortunes of two funds whose managers selected and adhered to different risk/return trade-offs. We'll assume that each has $10 million to invest. In this scenario one manager, Caroline, feels she is under intense political pressure to avoid having to report an unrealized loss as required by GASB 31. Her strategy, then, is to buy 3-month T-bills and automatically reinvest in the same as they mature. The other manager, Karl, is less wary of GASB 31; his advisory board members know the difference between realized and unrealized losses—and prefer a higher return. With their support, Karl invests entirely in 2-year USTNs, reinvesting proceeds in the same maturity as each bond matures. Caroline and Karl hold to their strategies for a full ten years, and they reinvest all coupons. (Note: The author does not endorse this strategy; it is used here strictly for illustration purposes.)

We know from the data in Exhibit 6-1 that Caroline is getting 54.80 percent of the return of the 30-year UST bond for only 15.99 percent of the risk; Karl is capturing 70.08 percent of that return for about 23.84 percent of the risk. The difference in annualized return, basis points, represents an opportunity cost to stakeholders in Caroline's fund. But how much is that? Exhibit 6-4, the Opportunity Cost Evaluator, tells the tale. Karl's fund ends up with $1,869,021 more than Caroline's over a ten-year period. This is what I like to refer to as the "GASB insurance premium" paid out by Caroline and her investment board. It makes one wonder: How many library books could have been purchased with $1.8 million? How many teacher's aides or firefighters could have been employed over ten years with that extra money? One hopes the people at the Governmental Accounting Standards Board are asking similar questions. GASB 31 is a reporting requirement designed to provide *bondholders*, not *taxpayers*, with insights into the financial health of public funds. It was not designed to influence investment strategy. Yet it does—and in most cases for the worse—as shown by our example.

EXHIBIT 6-4
THE OPPORTUNITY COST EVALUATOR

	3-Month T-Bill	2-Year Treasury
Avg of 1Yr Returns for 10Yr Period	4.34	5.55
Future Value 10Yrs Forward	$15,293,551	$17,162,572
Opportunity Cost (basis points)	121	
Opportunity Cost (actual dollars)	$1,869,01	

Yes, the 3-month T-bill strategy carries a heavy opportunity cost. Assuming the investment plan for liquidity is in place, the only benefit to incurring that cost is the avoidance of a mark-to-market loss if interest rates rise. But is the benefit proportionate to the cost? Take a look at the calculations in Exhibit 6-5 and be the judge. Here we've calculated the worst-case one-time account period loss for Karl's portfolio, juxtaposing it to the opportunity cost that Caroline's fund would incur in choosing her 3-month T-bill strategy over Karl's strategy based on higher-paying 2-year USTNs.

EXHIBIT 6-5
COST/BENEFIT COMPARISON:
WORST-CASE ACCOUNTING PERIOD LOSSES

		Worst-case accounting loss	1.8 million opportunity cost on a $10 million portfolio is:
If interest rates rose . . .	100 basis points	($190,000)	9.8 times the accounting loss
	200 basis points	($375,000)	4.9 times the accounting loss
	300 basis points	($560,000)	3.3 times the accounting loss

According to this analysis, a 100 basis point (1 percent) rise in interest rates would produce a temporary accounting loss of $190,000 for Karl's fund, but Caroline is giving up almost 10 times that amount in *real dollars* by staying short. One has to ask, Should the fear of a $1 paper loss cost taxpayers $9.80 in real money? Where is the fiduciary responsibility in that? Even under the unlikely scenario of a 300 basis point interest-rate rise, Caroline is taking an opportunity loss 3.3 times greater than a paper loss in her portfolio holdings. This represents the high price of allowing the fear of GASB 31 reported losses to dictate your investment strategy.

For the fund manager, determining the opportunity cost of staying excessively short has great value in that it quantifies the economic cost of that choice. The manager can say, "Here's the cost. Is it worth that much to you?" Opportunity cost can also be used to educate board members about other trade-offs, both economic and political.

THE TAX BITE

We have represented opportunity cost as the cost to the fund of forgoing some alternative. But there is yet another way to look at it: as a tax bite on citizens, since every dollar of opportunity cost affects citizens in the form of added or higher taxes or reduced public services.

One way to quantify the impact of opportunity cost on citizens is to answer this question: How many additional tax dollars would we have to raise in order to produce income equal to dollars lost through GASB 31 avoidance or some other excuse for not optimizing the portfolio? Returning to Caroline's portfolio as an example, we can see that her strategy of choosing 3-month T-bills over 2-year USTNs is shortchanging returns by 121 basis points per year on her $10 million portfolio. She is leaving $121,000 on the table every year at current rates.

So, our question is this: Assuming that Caroline can continue to earn 4.34 percent on principal invested in 3-month T-bills, what amount of principal (i.e., taxpayers' money) is needed to produce an additional $121,000 each year? The formula, which we must solve for x.

$$\frac{\text{OPPORTUNITY COST}}{\text{T-BILL}} = \text{TAXES}$$

$$\frac{\$121,000}{0.0434} = \$2,788,018$$

In other words, the principal amount of Caroline's portfolio would have to be increased by more than 25 percent—from $10 million to $12,788,018—to obtain the same dollar return that Karl is already getting from his $10 million portfolio. When explained in this way, the decision has greater relevance for both the politicians and the public.

Exhibit 6-6 on the next page, the Performance Enhancement Table (PET), is designed as a shortcut you can use to illustrate the risk/return

EXHIBIT 6-6
PERFORMANCE ENHANCEMENT TABLE (PET)

Portfolio Size	$10,000,000	$10,000,000	$10,000,000
Enhanced Basis Points	100	125	121 (2-year USTN yield less 3-month T-bill yield)
Enhanced Cash Flow	$100,000	$125,000	$121,000
Portfolio Yield			
3.75%	$2,666,667	$3,333,333	$3,226,666
4.00%	$2,500,000	$3,125,000	$3,025,000
4.34%	$2,304,147	$2,880,184	$2,788,018
4.50%	$2,222,222	$2,777,778	$2,688,888
4.75%	$2,105,263	$2,631,579	$2,547,368

trade-off. For a portfolio of $10 million, you can show your investment committee or council how much in taxation would be needed in order to produce the enhanced cash flow. The table gives the practitioner the ability to put in his own assumptions about the return rates of investment. Is your current strategy producing an opportunity cost? If it is, use the PET table (or the formula method used above) to determine how many additional taxpayer dollars you'd need to make up the difference on a sustained basis.

STRATEGY VERSUS TACTICS

In ending this chapter, we would like to clarify one point: The risk/return and maturity optimization we've described here represents a portfolio-level policy strategy. This strategy, however, should not preclude the fund manager from "tactical" moves aimed at making adjustments to the portfolio's overall maturity, or opportunistically enhancing returns. For example, a manager following this strategy might, as a tactic, sell a callable bond and replace it with a noncallable alternative if he anticipates a call and the likelihood of reinvesting at a lower rate. A sound strategy augmented by professionally executed tactics produces winning results on both economic and political fronts. The same cannot be said for tactics alone. So give your attention to both.

THE POWER OF GOOD COMMUNICATION

A great portfolio manager isn't simply a savvy investor. He or she is also an effective communicator, capable of quantifying trade-offs, as we've shown here, and explaining their implications to investment board members and the public. Communication, in fact, is one of the most valuable weapons in the fund manager's arsenal. Communication can and should be used to gain support for strategies that optimize income within constraints of suitable investing behavior. Here are just a few communication opportunities:

- Educate officials and the public on the difference between realized and unrealized mark-to-market losses. Doing so can neutralize the perverse influence of GASB 31 on the manager's efforts to optimize portfolio income. This may be the best way to avoid leaving money on the table. Officials and the public need to understand the very real opportunity costs of avoiding unrealized losses.
- Educate fund stakeholders about strategies that produce higher income and the opportunity costs of not pursuing them. Then quantify the impacts on fund income. The easy part of the manager's job is buying bonds; the hard part is explaining why.
- Help fund officials understand the *real* risk differences between allowable classes of securities. Then show them the income differences produced by those securities.

POINTS TO REMEMBER

- Historical data can be used to quantify the trade-off between risk (in terms of standard deviation) and return. The measurement can then be used to optimize income in the portfolio.
- Opportunity cost is the value of an alternative not taken. When managers invest short term simply to avoid reporting unrealized losses (per GASB 31), they inflict an opportunity cost on their funds.
- Once you've calculated the opportunity cost of unnecessarily short-term investment, you can use the figure to educate fund stakeholders about the costs of their decisions.
- Another way to educate stakeholders on opportunity cost is to calculate the amount that taxpayers would have to contribute to investment principal in order to generate the income of an investment alternative not taken.

CHAPTER 7

Profiting from Losses

You won't improve your results by pulling out the flowers and watering the weeds.

—PETER LYNCH

KEY POINTS COVERED IN THIS CHAPTER

- How taking gains reduces budget income
- The problem with discount and premium bonds
- How realizing losses and using the proceeds to rebalance the portfolio can put you ahead

Congratulations! Some of the bonds in your portfolio are now worth more than what you paid for them. Perhaps it's time to cash in your chips and take a nice profit. You'll surely get a pat on the back. But what would you do with the proceeds? Chances are your bond values rose because interest rates dropped, which means your reinvestment rate might be lower. So what should you do?

Even though your bonds are now in positive territory, there will surely be times when rising interest rates will create mark-to-market losses. What to do? Sell and take a loss so you can reinvest at the higher rate? The very thought of deliberately realizing a loss gives you a funny feeling in your stomach. You're beginning to think the buy-and-hold strategy of just ignoring these fluctuations and doing nothing may be best. After all, isn't that what most public fund managers do?

This chapter tackles a number of thorny issues confronting portfolio managers who identify themselves as investors—that is, neither as traders, who aim to enhance returns from price changes, nor as buy-and-hold managers, who deliberately ignore changes in market conditions. It will:

- Dispel the notion that gains are always good and losses are bad
- Point to situations in which selling a security before maturity is both the prudent and responsible thing to do
- Demonstrate why making the distinction between accounting loss and economic loss is essential

Above all, the chapter offers a better alternative to what most public fund managers do: sell their gains and hold their losses. That may seem counterintuitive to you. If it does, read on.

HOW GAINS CREATE PAIN

Plautus, the Roman comic playwright, told us that "There are occasions when it is undoubtedly better to incur loss than to make gain." Few in the public fund world would agree. This section aims to change minds.

We begin by asking, What is a gain? As is so often the case with portfolio management, Wall Street and Main Street have different interpretations of the same form. Wall Street and accountants define a *gain* as the difference between original cost or book value of a security and its market value excluding accrued interest. So if you sold a security for more than you booked it, the difference excluding accrued interest would be your gain. Accrued interest is ignored because at settlement—the date the money and security actually change hands—the buyer will pay the seller the market price plus any accrued interest due the seller. The buyer will be repaid the amount of accrued interest on the next coupon payment date.

Main Street defines gain in the same way but sees a different implication in terms of the income available to the budget. (More on this a bit later.) In the world of gain and loss, Main Street is concerned with its two forms of principal: political and economic. Recalling our earlier discussions, political principal is analogous to the egg-laying goose and economic principal refers to her eggs. To examine the impact of what happens when gains are realized on Main Street, consider a town with a one-bond portfolio. Muddville owns a $1 million U.S. Treasury note (USTN) that has a 5-year maturity and a coupon of 4 percent. It was purchased at par (100). The purchase yield of this note will produce $40,000 (two semi-annual coupon payments of $20,000 each), which is set aside for the budget. At the end of the first year, rates have fallen one percent so a USTN with four years remaining to maturity now yields 3 percent. That rate drop raised the market value of the portfolio's note to 103.75, giving the fund a recognized but unrealized gain of $37,500. There is joy in Muddville!

If the portfolio manager sells this note and realizes his gain at the very beginning of the second year, his one-year holding period return will be 7.75 percent. That return comes from the $40,000 received in coupons during first year plus the $37,500 gain on the sale. The manager will then have $1,037,500 in cash and a realized return of 7.75 percent. But what should he do next? He has more political principal than he started with (a fatter goose), but is faced with a lower reinvestment rate, which could spell less economic principal (a smaller clutch of eggs) in the years ahead. Perhaps this manager sold thinking rates had hit bottom at 3 percent and would begin to rise. That would be a perfect ending, but we live in an imperfect world. So let's say rates don't rebound and our manager has to reinvest at 3 percent, buying a 4-year USTN (the same number of years left on the note he just sold) at par yielding 3 percent.

What's the net impact of all this? For public funds it is important to understand that gains represent some of the future income (eggs) received today. In reality what happens is that the eggs are not spent but swapped for a bigger goose ($1,037,500 instead of $1 million) and less egg production per pound of goose at 3 percent versus the previous 4 percent. Has our manager made a good move? Consider the alternatives:

Alternative A: Do nothing
$1,000,000 at 4% = $40,000 a year for five years
Total income over five years = $200,000

Alternative B: Sell after year 1 and reinvest at 3%
$1,000,000 at 4% = $40,000 for the first year
$1,037,500 at 3% = $31,125 times 4 years = $124,500 for years 2 through 5
Total income = $40,000 + $124,500 = $164,500

Alternative A produced $200,000 for the budget without touching the original investment (political principal). Alternative B produced $164,500, $35,500 less. Note, however, that in addition to the income shortfall, $37,500 has been moved from economic principal to political principal and is not available to the current budget for income. (One could still budget $40,000 per year but doing so would require the sale of $4,433.75 every six months—hardly a practical solution.)

Now you might think, "At maturity the manager who sold and booked the gain will start with $37,500 more political principal than his nonselling counterpart. With that greater principal going to work, it can't take long to get back to equal in terms of total income, right?" Let's take a look. Over four years the fund has forgone $35,500 of budget income. Let's say that rates have returned to 4 percent. So the manager who did nothing—let's call him Manager A—has $1 million to invest at 4 percent while Manager B has $ 1,037,500 of political principal (original political principal plus realized gain) available to do the same. Manager A earns $40,000 per year while B earns $41,500—or $1,500 more for each year. Even with this greater income it will take Manager B almost 24 years to recover from taking the realized gains!

> Note: Keep in mind the only way Manager B can come out without touching political principal of $1,037,500 is to either budget for 3 percent, or budget for 4 percent but acknowledge that the cash flow from this position will not be sufficient to pay obligations without selling a portion of the security. Selling will subject the portfolio to a principal loss if rates are not at 3 percent when sale is made. This must be repeated for the remaining four years. Another option is to sit on the gains in cash at money market rates until rates rise to levels above 3 percent. This, however does not really solve the budget problem unless proceeds from sales are reinvested at 3.95 percent or higher.

Our tale of the two managers has demonstrated what happens to public funds as managers sell securities only when they have gains, a too-frequent pattern of behavior. Managers who follow this practice can point to increases in principal, but they end up being short on income and wondering why. **They don't realize continued profit-taking can, paradoxically, reduce the income they need for their budgets.** And they ask themselves, "Why am I losing the budget game when I'm winning the investment game?" Hopefully our illustration has explained why, and will motivate you to rethink the current practices of taking gains and holding losses.

WHERE DID THE GAIN ON SALE GO?

Gains must be categorized as realized or unrealized. Realized gains from the sale of a security should not be confused with recognized but *un*realized gains shown in financial reports. Realized gains occur when a security is sold above its purchase price; the proceeds from the sale are then reinvested. Unrealized gains are simply reported. It is seldom understood that, depending on the size of the gain, taking gains can make the goose bigger but actually reduce egg production, as we've seen. Yet traders—those managers who actively sell securities before maturity—look to gains as their primary source of spendable income. For them, the boundary between principal and income is not neatly defined. Budgeting is problematic for them owing to the uncertainty surrounding trading strategies, which may fail to deliver. To avoid selling a security to meet budgeted obligations, that uncertainty is usually managed by substantially understanding the income forecast. Thus, instead of starting with a budget of, say, 4 percent, traders would pick 3 percent.

HOW TO PROFIT FROM TAKING LOSSES

Losses are always bad—that's the conventional wisdom. Unrealized paper losses create political problems for the public officials. Realized losses on investments are even more painful since they reduce the size of fund principal. Using our analogy, a loss shrinks the goose, and a small goose cannot produce as many eggs as a large one, all other factors being equal. Yet taking losses is usually preferable to taking gains. That statement will strike you as counterintuitive, but it's true, and this section will show you why. Here are its underlying reasons:

- A public fund manager should be willing to consider rebalancing the portfolio throughout all market cycles. The goal is to keep portfolio income at levels equal to the current market, something we don't often see because managers are reluctant to realize losses.

- Portfolio managers should feel comfortable maintaining a market rate of return through changing market cycles—even if it means realizing a loss. Doing so is consistent with the investment policy's goal of principal preservation and keeps the portfolio in a position to create the greatest benefit for taxpayers.
- Managers should understand premium, par, and discount securities. Public funds typically shy away from securities priced at a premium for two reasons: they think paying the higher price means they're getting a bad deal; and the accounting treatment creates problems at maturity for funds that don't use a *constant yield* calculation. (Note: The author is not advocating either taking or not taking losses. He is merely pointing out that many portfolio strategies are impacted and dictated not by strategy but by fear of public and political perceptions.)

Not All Losses Are Created Equal

The first thing to understand about profiting from losses is the difference between a *liquidation loss* and an *investment loss*. A liquidation loss permanently removes money from the portfolio. For example, a fund may have to liquidate $2 million in bonds to pay for a planned renovation of several school buildings. An investment loss, on the other hand, will temporarily reduce the size of portfolio. It may cost the goose some weight and some of her egg production, at least for a time. But under solid portfolio management, she will eventually recover her weight loss and move on to a higher level of egg production.

Premium, Par, and Discount Bonds

Before we describe specific examples of how you can profit from taking a loss, we need to brush up on the differences between *premium, par,* and *discount* bonds. Exhibit 7-1 summarizes those differences.

Few public fund portfolio managers buy premium bonds because these bonds confuse the distinction between principal and income when accounting for results. As noted earlier, because the investor pays a higher price—say, 108.53 versus 100—many investment managers or their politi-

EXHIBIT 7-1
PREMIUM, PAR, AND DISCOUNT BONDS

Premium	A bond that sells for more than its face value	Example: A $1 million bond selling for $1,037,500. The coupon on a premium bond is higher than a market coupon given the same quality and maturity.
Par	A bond selling at its face (or par) value. Face value is the value of the bond at maturity.	Example: a bond selling for $100,000 that is redeemable at maturity for $100,000.
Discount	A bond selling for less than its face value.	Example: a bond redeemable for $100,000 selling for $99,125.

A COMMENT ABOUT GASB 31 AND MARK-TO-MARKET

GASB 31 ignores book value and looks only at ending market value minus beginning market value plus coupons received or interest earned. The calculation is actually more complicated and we would refer the reader to the GASB 31 booklet for the specific calculation. The point is that GASB 31 does not differentiate between a change in market value and cash flow. The public fund does not have this luxury. It has to be able to do two things GASB 31 ignores. First, provide a stable budget—one whose payment of obligations would not require the fund to sell the security. Second, it must demonstrate if called upon that principal remains intact when realizing a loss.

As we have pointed out, public funds are directed to possess some level of risk in pursuit of an appropriate rate of return for the investment portfolio. This will inevitably produce a loss when rates rise. So while GASB 31 does not differentiate between recognized and realized losses, the public funds must differentiate if they are to budget effectively and still be accountable to the taxpayer who demands principal preservation. *Profiting from taking losses moves from recognized and unrealized losses to realized losses. This process requires the public fund manager be prepared to explain how the political principal can remain intact if a realized loss is incurred.*

---

cal overseers think they have paid too much. Additionally, since bonds mature at 100 (par), some public funds will show a loss of principal at maturity because they do not amortize the premium during the holding period. For example, if you invested 108.53 for a bond that paid 100 at maturity, you'd appear to have incurred a principal loss of 8.53 percent. Both perceptions, however, are mistaken. Higher price does not imply the fund is paying too much for the same yield, nor is there a real loss of principal at maturity. The higher price is a result of receiving an above-market coupon; for example, the public fund is receiving an 8 percent coupon when the market is currently paying 6 percent. Instead of reducing the price or amortizing, the fund recognizes the whole coupon as income. The breakdown should be 6 percent income and 2 percent return of principal. The 2 percent return of principal is what reduces the price as the bond goes through maturity.

Prior to the issuance of GASB 31, a common practice among funds—and one some funds still practice—was to keep the book price unchanged until maturity. When these funds purchased a premium bond they would treat the above-market coupon or investment cash flow as income. At maturity, the entire premium would be written down in a single stroke. So for the first fours years the fund overstated income by an amount equal to the above-market coupon. Since the income in the last year is only 6 percent and the premium write-down is 8.53 percent it appears on paper as a principal loss. That, in the author's opinion, explains why public funds before and after GASB 31 continue to shy away from premium bonds.

To appreciate the choices faced by a fund in deciding whether to purchase premium, par, or discount bonds, consider Exhibit 7-2. Here we have three actual bonds with the same five-year maturity. These bonds have only two things in common: purchase yield (yield to maturity, or YTM), and the $1 million dollars that each investor has put into them.

The Premium Bond

Consider the premium bond, bond A. If you owned it you would be receiving 8 percent on the par amount of $921,402. The amount of a U.S. Treasury note with a 6 percent yield your $1 million could purchase is:

EXHIBIT 7-2
A TALE OF THREE BONDS

Bond	Purchase Yield	Coupon	Principal Invested	Price	Face Amount	Annual Cash Flow
A (Premium)	6%	8%	$1,000,000	108.53	$921,402	$73,712
B (Par)	6%	6%	$1,000,000	100.00	$1,000,000	$60,000
C (Discount)	6%	4%	$1,000,000	91.47	$1,093,257	$43,730

$921,402 \times 1.0853 = \$1$ million. The annual cash flow from this premium bond would be $73,712. At the end of the fifth and final year the bond would mature at 100, or $921,402. But, alas, you had invested $1 million. What happened to the $78,598 of principal ($1 million invested less $921,402 returned)? The answer is that it was spent—a fact that the mathematics of yield to maturity has concealed.

The math of yield to maturity (YTM) assumes all cash flows from the investment are reinvested at the same rate. Thus, the 6 percent YTM assumes you've reinvested each of your semi-annual coupon payments at 6 percent. Being a public fund, you didn't do this; instead, you put that coupon income into the budget for current spending. Yes, you received 8 percent each year ($73,712) on your $921,402 face value bond. In essence you were receiving 8 percent on $921,402, not 6 percent on $1 million. The difference is $73,712 − $60,000 = $13,712. Over five years, that amounts to $68,560 or $5,152 short of the $73,712 figure. That difference can be accounted for in the interest you could have earned but *didn't* earn because you spent your coupons instead of reinvesting them.

The next chapter on *duration* deals with this problem in depth and shows why all the securities in Exhibit 7-2 earn exactly the same amount. Suffice to say that buying premium bonds creates headaches for the public fund manager. There is much to be explained and much to be accounted for—and few fund stakeholders or members of the public would understand these explanations in any case. For some managers, the benefits of premium bonds, in fact, rarely offset the accounting headaches they create for fund managers.

The Discount Bond

Discount bonds have the opposite problem. In our example, the 4 percent coupon on bond C is below the current market offering of 6 percent. Consequently, the $1 million investment will buy $1,093,257 of face value. Again, there is no magic: the below-market coupon, 4 percent instead of the current market rate of 6 percent, translates into a lower price: a $1 million bond at maturity costs only $914,700 today (or $1 million buys, at a 91.47 dollar price, a $1,093,257 face amount for a 5-year 4 percent USTN). The pricing mechanism, in effect, makes yield-oriented investors indifferent to available choices.

With $1,093,257 at 4 percent, bond C's owner is on the receiving end of an annual cash flow of about $43,730. That's much less than the $60,000 she would have received if she had selected the par bond, bond B. Even though she is receiving a 6 percent yield to maturity, a portion will not be received until maturity. If the owner had budgeted at the purchase yield of 6 percent she would find herself short by $17,270 ($60,000 − $43,730) every year until the bond was redeemed. At redemption she'd receive $1,093,257, an amount well above the $1 million she initially invested. The extra redemption proceeds, in effect, are the interest income shortfall resulting from the 4 percent coupon instead of 6 percent during the preceding years. Her goose would be returned much larger. But this does not solve the problem of the cash shortfall in the period prior to redemption. The question for public fund managers who have current obligations to meet is this: How can cash shortfalls in the early years be made up?

In the real world of public fund investing, there is no good answer to this question. Consequently, managers avoid owning all premium bonds or deep discount bonds and instead gravitate to bonds priced relatively close to par. The few they do hold are priced so close to par they do not materially impact the income and cash flow of the fund.

Bond fund managers on Wall Street are unhampered by the issues that make premium and discount bonds problematic for their cousins on Main Street. Wall Street is concerned with primarily one thing: total return. Except in rare cases, its practitioners do not have to worry about assuring a steady, budgeted income stream. As readers certainly know, the situation on Main Street is much different, and that difference complicates budgeting and portfolio strategy for public funds. This is regrettable since discount and premium bonds often present opportunities to reduce either interest-rate risk or reinvestment risk. In fact, the problems associated with these bonds are often the source of those opportunities.

PROFITING FROM LOSSES: AN ILLUSTRATED CASE

Fortunately, there is a way to take a loss and come out ahead: Rebalance the portfolio to maintain the appropriate rate of return through market cycles. Realizing losses can be a suitable strategy for maintaining portfolio yield during market cycles, assuming adequate liquidity has been established and the public fund's management understands both the political and economic issues. In this section we'll show you how. But first, some important definitions:

Take-out yield   The minimum yield required to replace or break even on the sale of a security. It is the market's break-even offer for the remaining cash flows on the political principal of the security. Some portfolio managers do not grasp the difference between a purchased yield—the price at which they bought the security, or its book price—and the current market yield, the value of the security based on its remaining cash flows.

Market yield   The yield *asked* or offered to a buyer.

Return pickup   A term that expresses in basis points the expected economic gain over a take-out yield after the return of principal. It is the profit above what would have been earned without realizing the loss.

We are now prepared to see what can be done to turn a realized loss into a gain for the public fund. Let's make these assumptions about the security being sold:

- A 2-year USTN of 1/31/04 yielding 3 percent was purchased at par and settled on 1/31/02.
- One year later, interest rates have risen 1 percent across the yield curve.
- The USTN is now underwater (has a book loss); if sold it would receive a 4 percent market bid.
- As of 1/31/03, a 4 percent bid on a USTN 3 percent of 1/31/04 equals a dollar price of 99.029. Note: Price is the present value of the remaining cash flows discounted at 4 percent.
- As of 1/31/03, the following US federal agency bond is offered:
    Issuer: FHLMC (Federal Home Loan Mortgage Corporation aka
       Freddie Mac)
    Maturity: 1/15/04
    Coupon: 3.25 percent
    Offer price: 98.83
    YTM: 4.50 percent

With a rise in rates, the portfolio manager recognizes an opportunity to improve his portfolio income. Doing so will involve realizing a loss: a political risk. "Someone will complain that I've lost principal," he thinks to himself. The following example will help readers understand how taking a loss to produce income is consistent with the obligation to both preserve principal and achieve an appropriate level of income. For this obligation to be fulfilled, the following conditions, one political and one economic, must be met:

- Political issue: safety of principal. The original principal is preserved, even though a book loss is realized.
- Economic issue: income. There is an economic advantage to realizing the book loss.

With these conditions in mind, let's examine the transaction.

- Sell: The portfolio manager sells the original 2-year, 3 percent USTN purchased at par on 1/31/2002. The sale takes place on 1/31/2003 at a take-out yield of 4 percent, at a price of 99.029.
- Buy: The proceeds of the sale are immediately reinvested into a 1-year, 3.25 percent FHLMC (Freddie Mac) bullet note with a maturity date of 1/15/2004. The market yield is 4.50 percent offered at a price of 98.83.

Now let's evaluate the transaction from Main Street's uniquely dual perspectives.

Political Evaluation

Priority one for every public fund manager is safety of principal—keeping the goose safe. This manager started with $1 million invested in a USTN for two years at 3 percent. That produced $30,000 annually for the budget. He paid 100, par, for the security. Now, one year later, rates have risen and the note's market value has slipped. If the note were liquidated, it would fetch an offered price of 99.029, or $990,290—creating a $9,710 loss on the original $1 million investment. But until a sale is actually made, this is only a paper loss—not a principal loss—and the fund continues earning its $30,000 in interest income.

This portfolio manager must be prepared to explain to superiors, officials, and the public how taking a loss will *not* create a principal loss. (In some situations the transaction may require approval in advance of execution.) And here's how he does it:

The Fund Manager has found an opportunity to improve the portfolio's income *and* stay within the budget and risk guidelines of the investment plan. He has sufficient liquidity to meet current obligations and is focused on keeping the portfolio yield at current market levels. As he tells the Investment Board, "By rebalancing the portfolio, we can increase the fund's income *and* preserve principal." Some board members appear skeptical. He projects a slide on the screen. The slide shows the consequences of selling the 2-year USTN at a yield of 4 percent.

Where We Now Stand

Realized Ending Value + Coupon		
$1,000,000 \times 99.029 =$		$ 990,290
One-year accrued interest =		30,000
One-year interest on interest =		238
Holding period proceeds =		$1,020,528
Original investment		1,000,000
Economic principal		$ 20,528
Purchase price	= 100.00	
Sale price	= 99.029	
Book loss	= 0.971	$ (9,707)

"As shown here, our 2-year USTN would fetch $990,290 if we sold today. We've already made $30,000 in interest from coupons, and another $238 in interest on coupon interest (30,000 invested at 3 percent for six months). So one year into the investment, we're $20,528 ahead."

One of the skeptics on the board chimes in. "Yes, but if you just leave things alone, we'd be $30,238 ahead. So why should we sell this note? A sale would cut into our principal."

From an accounting perspective, the board member has a point. But accounting, fortunately, has little to do with economics. When bills have to be paid, and when money needs to be invested, it's economic values, not accounting values that matter.

Economic Evaluation

From an accounting perspective, the fund has lost principal. The economic reality, however, is that the fund is ahead by $20,528 after one year. That's a bit short of the $30,000 gain the manager had hoped for when he purchased the USTN, but it beats being in negative territory.

So where can our fund manager go from here? Can he turn a lemon into lemonade? The answer is yes, if he takes the following steps: sell the USTN, book the loss, and use the proceeds to rebalance the portfolio. Doing so will produce a better budget outcome for future years while preserving principal. This can be accomplished even if the fund has already spent its earned coupon income—as most do. Here's how: use the sale proceeds to purchase another security at a take-out yield *above* that of the security being liquidated. Remember the take-out yield is the minimum yield necessary for the fund to both preserve principal and earn the same income as the initial investment would have earned over the remaining time to maturity.

Let's return to the case.

The Fund Manager has a commitment to produce 3 percent for the year on $1 million, or $30,000. So here is what he tells his board. "I am going to sell our $1 million T-note and buy a Freddie Mac with essentially the same maturity, but with a 4.5 percent yield to maturity. This will not only earn back our $9,707 T-note loss, but will deliver an interest rate that *exceeds* the annual $30,000 we need to meet our budget."

Is this possible? Let's evaluate what the fund manager is proposing. First, he plans to sell the 3 percent USTN of 1/31/2004 for $990,290. He will use those proceeds to buy a $1 million face value Freddie Mac agency note of 1/15/2004 with a 3.25 percent coupon. In doing so he will be replacing the full faith and credit of the federal government (USTN) with the implicit backing of the federal government (Freddie Mac). Once that transaction is completed, the fund will own a security earning 4.5 percent, or 50 basis points higher than the take-out yield. For the coming year, this will produce an additional $5,000 in income with a 15-day shorter maturity (1/15/2004 versus 1/31/2004). A $5,000 income enhancement on $30,000 translates into almost a 17 percent improvement in income in exchange for a marginally altered credit risk while keeping the interest-rate risk unchanged. Not a bad day's work for this fund manager.

A CLOSER LOOK

Would you like to know more about this fund manager's rebalancing strategy? Let's look at the economics in detail.

The proceeds from sale of the USTN amounted to $990,290. The fund manager then bought the agency note for $988,320 with the balance of his cash going to $1,444 accrued interest and $546 cash take-out. Exhibit 7-4 (page 105) indicates that if the manager did nothing until the 1/15/2004 maturity date of the USTN, the fund would earn $1,028,985. By realizing

EXHIBIT 7-3
BOOK LOSS IS NOT A PRINCIPAL LOSS

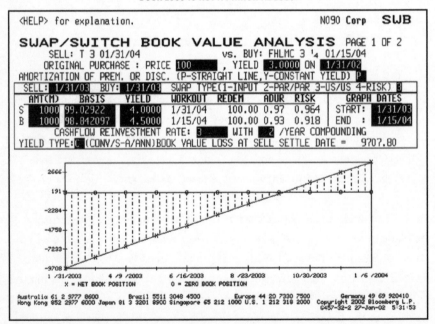

the loss and immediately reinvesting in the agency, the fund earned $1,033,414, about $4,428 more income. The amount is slightly less than $5,000 only because the rebalancing was made to a security with a 15-day shorter maturity. (The USTN had a maturity of 1/31/2004 while the agency maturity was 1/15/2004.)

Exhibit 7-3 indicates when the political principal is recovered through the rebalance strategy. Where the lines cross shows when and by how much the rebalance strategy adds value. The transaction was initiated in January 2003, and the full principal was recovered in approximately nine months.

Exhibit 7-4 shows from differing perspectives the actual results of using only the proceeds from the sale to optimize income and minimize loss.

Where Exhibit 7-3 showed the investment committee how long it would be until the loss and original income was recovered, Exhibit 7-4 focused on the additional income produced by the rebalance strategy. Think of 7-3 as the political perspective and 7-4 as the economic perspective.

EXHIBIT 7-4
PRESERVE PRINCIPAL, INCREASE INCOME

<HELP> for explanation.			N090 Corp **SW**		
SWAP/SWITCH ANALYSIS				Page 2 of 3	
SELL:T 3 01/31/04		vs BUY:FHLMC 3 ¼ 01/15/04			
AT SETTLEMENT DATE			SCENARIO		
CASHFLOW COMPONENTS	SELL BOND	BUY BOND	SELL:	1000M on 1/31/03	
PRINCIPAL	990,290	988,320	P/Y:99.029	/ 4.000	
ACCRUED INTEREST	0	1,444	BUY:	1000M on 1/31/03	
TAXES PAID ON B.V.	---	0	P/Y:98.832	/ 4.511	
SELL BEFORE BUY EARNS	---	0	REVIEW ON 1/15/04		
TAKEOUT	---	525	$ P/Y:99.998216 / 3.000		
			B P/Y:100	/ 3.250	
NET PRESENT VALUE	990,290	990,290	REINVEST 2/YR @ 4.500		
AT REVIEW DATE			DIFFERENCES		
INTEREST PAID OUT	15,000	32,500	17,500		
ACCRUED INTEREST	13,695	0	-13,695		
PRINCIPAL PAID OUT	0	0	0		
REINVESTMENT INCOME	307	365	57		
FV OF TAKEOUT	---	548	548		
REVIEW PRINCIPAL	999,982	1,000,000	17		
NET FUTURE VALUE	1,028,985	1,033,414	**4,428**		
TOTAL RETURN	**4.05**	**4.51**	46BP		

Australia 61 2 9777 8600   Brazil 5511 3048 4500   Europe 44 20 7330 7500   Germany 49 69 920410
Hong Kong 852 2977 6000 Japan 81 3 3201 8900 Singapore 65 212 1000 U.S. 1 212 318 2000   Copyright 2002 Bloomberg L.P.
G457-32-2 27-Jan-02 5:40:51

• • •

You can't be in the business of managing public funds for long without recognizing some paper gains and losses on your fixed income portfolio. It's part of the business because interest rates go up and down. If you're tempted to grab gains when the tide is with you, this chapter should have given you pause. And what about when the tide goes against you and you're faced with paper losses? Do you simply hold on? Hopefully, this chapter has demonstrated that you have a suitable option: to sell, take your losses, but then rebalance with securities that can—in the long run—put you and your fund ahead of the game.

POINTS TO REMEMBER

- Because most gains are caused by declines in market interest rates, taking a gain will force a manager to reinvest at those lower rates, reducing cash flow and future budgets.
- Funds should look for rebalancing opportunities in bull and bear markets. **The goal of rebalancing is to keep portfolio earnings at market rates of return throughout budget and economic cycles.**
- Premium and discount bonds generally create accounting headaches for fund managers.
- To benefit from taking a loss, use the sale proceeds to simultaneously purchase another security at a take-out yield *above* that of the security being liquidated.

CHAPTER 8

Understanding and Applying Duration

It's taken all my life to understand that it is not necessary to understand everything.

— RENÉ COTY

KEY POINTS COVERED IN THIS CHAPTER

- Average life is a flawed measure of price volatility
- Duration is the superior measure
- The weakness of yield to maturity as a management tool
- The use of duration in portfolio decisions

Managing interest-rate risk is a challenge for public fund managers. The challenge is even more formidable when we consider that many of these managers have limited time, resources, and staff. As a result, they need an understandable and practical way to apply the latest interest-rate risk management concepts.

This chapter addresses two of these concepts: *average life* and *duration*. Average life is simple and straightforward. It indicates when the investor's principal will be repaid. But this crude measure is of limited value. It is a tool portfolio managers should put in the closet, or minimize its use. Duration is a more robust approach to measuring the price volatility of fixed-income securities. Duration is based on mathematical formulas for which many readers may be unprepared. Thus, our chapter will be more about the meaning and application of duration than about its calculation.

The duration of particular bonds can, in any case, be found on dealer offering sheets, and software is also available for making calculations. (Microsoft Excel also has a "modified" duration calculation formula; this is fine for bullet bonds, but not for callable bonds or bonds with optionality.) Our objective here is to explain the logic of duration, why it is superior to the traditional idea of average life, and how you can use duration in managing portfolios.

Several books have influenced the material developed throughout this and the next chapter. They are the *The Handbook of Fixed Income Securities* by Frank Fabozzi, *Bond Risk Analysis* by Livingston Douglas, and *An Introduction to Option-Adjusted Spread Analysis* by Tom Windas. Readers who want to learn more about the calculation of duration and its application in portfolio management should consult these sources. The Web site, Investopedia.com, also has good material on duration.

DURATION TO THE RESCUE

Managers are obliged to evaluate bonds on several dimensions: creditworthiness, yield, the size and timing of coupons, purchase price, and—the issue that concerns us here—their price volatility in the face of changing market interest rates. Both average life and duration are used to measure the price volatility of fixed-income securities and the portfolios that contain them. Unfortunately, average life fails in this task. Consider the case of a portfolio manager who has $1 million to invest and is trying to decide which of four U.S. Treasury notes should be purchased (see Exhibit 8-1). Each note will mature in exactly five years—which is to say each has a 5-year life. All carry the full faith and credit guarantee of the U.S. government, so there is no difference in creditworthiness. And all are calculated to

EXHIBIT 8-1
FOUR DIFFERENT NOTES

	Coupon	Maturity	YTM	Price
A	0%	31 Oct 05	6%	74.40
B	4%	31 Oct 05	6%	91.46
C	6%	31 Oct 05	6%	100.00
D	8%	31 Oct 05	6%	108.53

have the same yield to maturity, 6 percent. And all are noncallable. While the characteristics that generally matter to portfolio managers are the same, there are differences: their prices, their coupon rates, and cash flows.

The portfolio manager new to public funds—and even seasoned practitioners—may be a little frustrated by the choices in Exhibit 8-1 since the most commonplace variables of interest (maturity, YTM, and credit risk) are exactly the same. So they are equivalent, right? Wrong. Differences in the size and timing of cash flows gives each of the four notes a unique price risk that the manager must consider.

Exhibit 8-2 profiles the cash flows of three of our T-notes: the 6 percent par note (Note C), and the notes with the greatest differences—the zero-coupon Note A, which is sold at a discount, and the 8 percent Note D, which sells at a premium. For simplicity, we assume annual coupon payments are made.

EXHIBIT 8-2
CASH FLOW PROFILES

Note	Investment	Year 1	Year 2	Year 3	Year 4	Year 5*
A (zero)	$1,000,000	0	0	0	0	$1,343,916
C (6%)	$1,000,000	$60,000	$60,000	$60,000	$60,000	$1,060,000
D (8%)	$1,000,000	$80,000	$80,000	$80,000	$80,000	$1,001,404**

* Note that the final year's cash flow includes both that year's interest (zero for Note A) as well as repayment of the face value of the note ($1 million).

** $80,000 for Year 5's coupon plus $921,402, which is the face amount of a $1 million investment made at 108.53.

The very different cash flow profiles shown in table 8-2 create much higher price volatility for Note A because the investor's cash flow comes entirely at maturity. It's back-end loaded. The entirety of the investor's reward is at risk of interest rate swings until the very end. As Marcia Stigum and Frank Fabozzi once put it, "The *lower* the coupon, the *greater* the percentage changes that will occur in a bond's price when rates rise or fall."[1] And you cannot find a bond with smaller coupons than a zero. In contrast, Note D has lower relative price risk and duration, because of its much higher coupon. Its owner is paid part of his yield to maturity with every passing year. Thus, less of his cash flow is subject to swings in interest rates.

Over the years, the author has witnessed citizens, politicians, investment committee members, and even finance directors and treasurers approach this type of situation with no appreciation that each of their choices contained a unique price risk. They frequently would use average life and price as the valuation yardstick. So looking at the above, if all three have the same yield of 6 percent, the same maturity or average life of five years, and all carry same credit guarantee of the U.S. government, then the one with the lowest price would seem the best buy. The problem is that not one of these facts tells us anything about the price volatility of the security. Worse, the same average life implies the same price risk.

The concept of duration comes to the rescue. There are several forms of duration. For now, we'll define *duration* as a measure of a bond's price volatility in the face of interest-rate changes. The higher the duration, the greater the security's price will change as interest rates change.

WHAT IS MEANT BY "DURATION"

There are several types of duration, each with a slightly different definition. When we refer here to duration, we mean "modified" duration, which represents the percentage price change for a given small change in interest rates, where small usually implies an instantaneous shift in rates plus or minus 100 basis points.[2] Rate shifts greater than 100 basis points would require us to go into the concept of convexity, which is beyond the scope of this book.

Duration provides the portfolio manager with a reliable means of quantifying the portfolio's expected change in value based on small changes in interest rates. As an example, let's suppose a bond priced at par has a dollar price of 100 with duration of 4.00. Should rates move up or down 1 percent (100 basis points), the price of the bond would be expected to change by 4 percent: to either 96 or 104, depending on the direction of the rate change. A bond with duration less than 4.00 would experience a smaller price swing under the same circumstance.

Now that you understand the duration concept, let's return to the four T-notes profiled in Exhibit 8-1 and answer the following questions.

Question 1: Does each of the four securities have the same interest-rate risk?

The answer is no. While all four T-notes share the same 6 percent yield, the same five-year average life, and same level of credit risk, each will produce a different set of cash flows for its owner. Those different cash flows will produce different levels of interest-rate risk. When interest rates change, the market value of these securities will not change by the same amount. The risk measure—modified duration—describes these differences. Higher duration translates into higher price volatility due to interest rate changes—and vice versa.

Question 2: How does duration affect portfolio strategy?

Durations can be calculated for bond portfolios as well as for individual bonds. Thus, the manager who wants to reduce interest-rate risk for an individual bond or for a portfolio of bonds should choose securities with lower duration.

AVERAGE LIFE VERSUS DURATION

Average life, as stated earlier, indicates when the investor's principal will be repaid. It entirely ignores the amounts and timing of coupons paid prior to principal repayment. Thus, the T-notes we've described in Exhibits 8-1 and 8-2 have average lives of five years.

Some managers think they can reduce interest-rate risk by reducing the weighted average maturity, or average life, of their portfolios. For example, reducing the average life from three years to two years, all other factors being equal, would reduce some of the price volatility of the portfolio. And a weighted average life is easy to calculate. But as we have seen, average life is not the only factor that impacts price volatility. Notes A, B, C, and D had the exact same maturities, but because of their different cash flow profiles, some were more volatile than others.

One of the most egregious errors of public fund management is the continued reliance on average life as a measure of interest-rate risk. An exception would be the use of average life to measure interest-rate risk for various mortgage-backed securities. Duration is a much more appropriate reflection of the portfolio's true interest-rate risk.

Why is average life such a poor measure of interest-rate risk? The simple answer is it ignores the time value of money. The time value of money recognizes that a dollar today is worth more than a dollar received sometime in the future. If you were given the choice of receiving a dollar today or receiving the same dollar one year from today, you'd choose today. Why? Time allows you to invest the dollar at an interest rate that will increase the value of your dollar. So, if you had a dollar today and could invest at, say, 10 percent (wouldn't that be nice?) for one year, then at maturity your one-year investment would grow to $1.10 (we will ignore interest-on-interest compounding for the moment and assume this is an annual, not semi-annual, period).

Another way to look at time value of money is that a dollar one year in the future is worth only about 91 cents today (to be exact, 90.91) if current one-year interest rates are 10 percent. (See "Present Value of One Dollar") This one-year rate is called the discount rate. The discount rate is the interest rate necessary to reduce a future dollar to its present value. In other words, a 10 percent discount rate is the rate needed to turn a future value of $1.00 into the present value of $0.9091. The concept of average life ignores this commonsense understanding of time value. All cash flows are equal in its eyes. Average life assumes a dollar received in one year is equal to a dollar received in five years. Average life isn't even interested in cash flows; its focus is entirely on the length of time to repayment of the original investment.

PRESENT VALUE OF ONE DOLLAR

Every textbook on investing or corporate finance contains a table indicating the present value of a dollar for different discount rates and over different time periods (years). A present value table indicates the effects of discount rates on the value of money received in the future. For instance, notice how the present value of $1.00 is $0.971 after one year at 3 percent, but drops to $0.935 at 7 percent. It also indicated the impact of time. For example, the dollar discounted at 7 percent over ten years is worth only $0.508!

For conciseness, we've abridged this table to a narrow range of discount rates and years.

Period (Years)	3%	4%	5%	6%	7%
1	0.971	0.962	0.952	0.943	0.935
2	0.943	0.925	0.907	0.890	0.873
3	0.915	0.889	0.864	0.840	0.816
4	0.889	0.855	0.823	0.792	0.763
5	0.863	0.822	0.784	0.747	0.713
6	0.838	0.790	0.746	0.705	0.666
7	0.813	0.760	0.711	0.665	0.623
8	0.789	0.731	0.677	0.627	0.582
9	0.766	0.703	0.645	0.592	0.544
10	0.744	0.676	0.614	0.558	0.508

The second problem with the average life approach: It ignores the magnitude of cash flows, not simply their timing. The size of cash flows is a critical component of interest-rate risk on a portfolio or security. Whenever interest rates change, the security's or portfolio's principal market value will change based on both the timing *and* the amount of cash flow generated. Portfolios with larger or smaller cash flows will react differently to interest rate changes. Using our earlier examples, the five-year average life of each security implies equal levels of interest-rate risk. This is profoundly inaccurate. Thus, using average life in lieu of duration in creating and managing portfolios can keep a fund manager in the dark with respect to price volatility.

PRICE VOLATILITY: A DEMONSTRATION

We've shown cash flow profiles are an effective way to understand how and why security prices are impacted by changes in interest rates and that duration, not average life, is the best yardstick for measuring it. But what magnitude of price volatility are we talking about? Let's revisit T-notes A, B, C, and D to find out. Exhibit 8-3 on the next page shows what can be expected to happen to the price of each of those T-notes when market interest rates change by either 1 percent or 2 percent, both up and down. Notice how the zero-coupon note (Note A) is the most affected. It increases in value by $102,480 when rates drop by 2 percent—more than any of the others. This price behavior explains why speculators buy zeros in anticipation of rate drops (yields lower, prices higher). The same bond, however, is hammered when market rates rise. Average life would not capture these changes and would lead a portfolio manager to believe each of the securities has the same interest-rate risk—a potential costly mistake.

EXHIBIT 8-3
ACTUAL PRICE VOLATILITY UNDER CHANGING MARKET RATE CONDITIONS
($1 MILLION INVESTMENT)

Note	Market Yield Change Coupon	−2%	−1%	+1%	+2%
A	0%	$102,480	$49,865	$(47,272)	$(92,098)
B	4%	$93,257	$45,416	$(43,126)	$(84,089)
C	6%	$89,826	$43,760	$(41,583)	$(81,109)
D	8%	$86,934	$42,365	$(40,283)	$(78,598)

LONG VERSUS SHORT MATURITIES

Our examples to this point have all had the same maturities: 5 years. By holding that factor constant, we've been able to talk about the impact of cash flows on duration and price volatility. But what would happen if we held other factors equal and simply changed the maturities? What we'd find is just what you'd expect: the price of long-term bonds is more volatile than the price of short-term bonds. Fortunately, the mathematics of duration takes years to maturity into consideration. So if you're looking at a 4-year bond with a duration of 3.2 and a 6-year bond with a duration of 3.2, you'll know their prices are equally susceptible to interest rate fluctuations.

DURATION FOR SECURITIES WITH UNCERTAIN CASH FLOWS

Up to this point we have been using *modified duration* to explain the duration concept. This is a measure of a bond's percentage change in price for a given absolute change in its yield. Modified duration is used to estimate the expected change in market value of the portfolio or security with small changes in interest rates (100 basis points or less). This measure works fine when noncallable bonds and portfolios of these bullet bonds are at issue. However, it is not useful for bonds that can be called away or whose cash flows could change (such as mortgage-backed bonds). In these cases, *effective duration* is the measure to use. Effective duration recognizes that yield changes may alter the expected cash flows. Effective duration is beyond the scope of this book.[3]

MACAULAY DURATION

We've now defined modified and effective duration. Modified duration is actually a derivative of an earlier measure called Macaulay duration, named after its originator. Macaulay conceived of duration as a measure of the effective life of a bond, but that measure can be modified to determine what concerns us in this chapter: the sensitivity of a bond's price to changes in the yield to maturity (or market interest rates). As described by Mark Kritzman, the modification simply requires we divide Macaulay duration by 1 plus the yield to maturity, as shown below:

$$\text{Modified duration} = \frac{D}{1 + YTM} \quad \text{where } D = \text{Macaulay duration}$$

Mark Kritzman, *The Portable Financial Analyst* (Charlottesville, VA: The Association for Investment Management and Research, 1995), 53.

USING DURATION IN PORTFOLIO DECISIONS

At this point, you're probably asking, "So how do I use this duration concept in building and managing my portfolio?" To answer the question, let's revisit the four T-notes described in Exhibits 8-1, 8-2, and 8-3. Which of the four should the portfolio manager consider purchasing? Remember, in seeking an answer the manager must keep price volatility low and satisfy a $60,000 per year budget.

All four have the same maturity, credit worthiness, and yield to maturity. They differ only in two respects: price and cash flow. Price is often used (mistakenly) as a method for making investment decisions. Faced with many securities with equal yields, some investors gravitate toward the lower-priced ones, thinking these represent greater value. By this yardstick, we should select the zero T-note since it has the lowest price. That would obviously be a bad choice in that it provides no money to the budget until maturity.

Duration can help us with the decision. Realizing higher duration means greater price fluctuation helps us to see our choices with new eyes. From the perspective of duration, the low-priced zero has the highest price risk. All things being equal, the prudent manager should choose the security with the least price volatility.

Cash flow should be another important consideration. The zero has no cash flow until maturity. There are only two ways to get cash out of a zero: hold it until maturity or sell it. But since zeros have the greatest price volatility, one may need to sell at a loss. So again, the zero is not a good choice for any fund that needs current income.

This leaves us with three remaining choices. Exhibit 8-4 revisits those choices, this time with their calculated durations. Let's look first at B and D, the 4 percent and 8 percent T-notes. If we choose the 4-percent, we would reduce the interest-rate risk, or duration, compared to the zero; we move to 4.42 from 4.85. But the substantial discount on this note means a good chunk of the YTM would be coming at maturity. Also, the note will not be producing the annual $60,000 in cash we may need for our budget, but only $40,000. The only way to cure the problem would be sell $20,000 pieces of the $1 million note at par each year to fund the shortfall—an unlikely prospect.

Now let's look at the Note D and its 8 percent coupon. Here we have the highest priced security with the lowest duration. On the plus side, this

EXHIBIT 8-4
THE FOUR T-NOTES REVISITED—WITH THEIR DURATIONS

	Coupon	Maturity	YTM	Price	Duration
A	0%	31 Oct 05	6%	74.40	4.85
B	4%	31 Oct 05	6%	91.46	4.42
C	6%	31 Oct 05	6%	100.00	4.26
D	8%	31 Oct 05	6%	108.53	4.12

note produces more cash flow than we need in our $60,000 budget. But there are negatives: The problem with this note is part of the annual cash flow is simply a return of the original premium paid at purchase. If we invested $1 million in this note, which was priced at 108.53 for each 100 of face value, we'll only receive $921,402 at maturity. Moreover, nearly $79,000 of the original or political principal will be returned before maturity and may not be spent in the budget. This can be confusing and difficult to track. Some heavy-duty accounting treatment will be needed to track our initial nest egg as the coupons roll in.

So the politically wise choice in an unchanged market would be Note C, the par 6 percent security. While it has a slightly higher duration than the 8 percent note, and lower duration than either the 4 percent note or zero, it has two likable features:

1. Its annual cash flow ($60,000) meets annual budget requirements. Nothing has to be sold to make up a cash shortfall; and
2. Being purchased at par, there are no accounting problems involving a return of principal with each coupon payment.

Now let's consider some other options. At this writing, the Federal Reserve has just completed its sixth increase in the federal funds rate, which has now moved from 1 percent to 2.5 percent and threatens to march higher. Oil is selling for more than $60 per barrel, near its historic peak. And the dollar has lost ground against the euro, making everything purchased from Europe more costly. The scent of inflation and higher interest rates is in the air.

In a scenario like this one, where higher rates threaten, should a public fund seek more cash flow and lower duration, or do just the opposite. The easy answer is the former: seek more cash flow with less price risk. More cash flow means the fund will have more money available to invest at higher interest rates, and lower duration means fewer worries about having to report paper losses because of GASB 31. That scenario would make Note D and its 8 percent coupon the security of choice among the four. The reverse would hold true if rates were expected to fall. In that case a fund would prefer to have less cash flow to reinvest at lower rates as long as cash was sufficient to meet budget requirements. In the case where rates are falling, having a security with above-market coupons would not be welcomed.

It is rare, of course, that a manager has a choice between securities like A, B, C, and D, which have identical maturities. In most cases the manager is looking at bonds with different prices, coupons, yields, *and* different maturities. Duration, fortunately, standardizes these different securities in terms of a key variable: price volatility. While exceptions exist in exotic structures, generally bonds with similar durations experience similar price fluctuations as interest rates change—even when their maturities differ.

DON'T BE MISLED BY YIELD TO MATURITY

Before we leave the subject of duration, we need to address one more common misunderstanding among Main Street fund managers: *yield to maturity (YTM)*. First, what does YTM really tell us? If you answered that yield to maturity is the interest rate or return that equates the present value of all future cash flows to today's bond price, you would be exactly right. YTM is the investment equivalent of the financial concept of internal rate of return, or IRR.

Now answer this question: Where does yield come from? Yield has three potential sources. With the exception of zeros and very deeply discounted bonds, the primary source of yield is usually the coupon. Depending on maturity, the second potential source of return is "interest on interest," or the amount of interest earned on the coupon payments. Last but not least in importance is the discount from or premium over the par price of the security. Thus, YTM has the following components of return:

1. Coupon return
2. Interest on interest return
3. +/- Price return

The point of describing YTM in this manner is to focus on the factors impacted when interest rates change. By identifying the various components of yield (return) we can better gauge how interest-rate risk will affect the security.

Many managers feel YTM is, next to the term of securities, the key number to consider in selecting securities and managing portfolios. Yield to maturity, however, contains an assumption some fund managers do not understand. The assumption, embedded in the mathematics of YTM, is that each cash flow (coupon) is reinvested at the same YTM. Thus, if you purchased a 5-year note with a YTM of 6 percent, the rate assumes you'll reinvest each semi-annual coupon payment *at that same rate* (6 percent), which is unlikely in an environment of fluctuating interest rates. Nor can you spend those coupons and expect your 6 percent rate of return to hold.

To appreciate how YTM can be "mis-yielding," (misleading), take a look at Exhibit 8-5, which examines a bond purchased at par with a 6 percent YTM under varying reinvestment or interest rate assumptions. Notice the last column, which has a zero reinvestment rate. Look down that column to the line titled "True Yield"—you'll see 5.32%. The lesson here is that spending coupons as they are received makes them unavailable for reinvestment, thus reducing the expected yield by 68 basis points from 6 percent to 5.32 percent.

EXHIBIT 8-5
WHY IS YTM A MIS-YIELDING TOOL?

The Yield to maturity calculation assumes all cash flows will be reinvested at the yield to maturity						
Semi-Annual Periods	Coupon 6%	Reinv Rate 8%	Reinv Rate 6%	Reinv Rate 4%	Reinv Rate 2%	Reinv Rate 0%
Par	$(1,000,000.00)	$0.00	$0.00	$0.00	$0.00	$0.00
0.5 yrs	$30,000.00	$0.00	$0.00	$0.00	$0.00	$0.00
1.0 yrs	$30,000.00	$1,200.00	$900.00	$600.00	$300.00	$0.00
1.5 yrs	$30,000.00	$2,448.00	$1,827.00	$1,212.00	$603.00	$0.00
2.0 yrs	$30,000.00	$3,745.92	$2,781.81	$1,836.24	$909.03	$0.00
2.5 yrs	$30,000.00	$5,095.76	$3,765.26	$2,472.96	$1,218.12	$0.00
3.0 yrs	$30,000.00	$6,499.59	$4,778.22	$3,122.42	$1,530.30	$0.00
3.5 yrs	$30,000.00	$7,959.57	$5,821.57	$3,784.87	$1,845.60	$0.00
4.0 yrs	$30,000.00	$9,477.95	$6,896.22	$4,460.57	$2,164.06	$0.00
4.5 yrs	$30,000.00	$11,057.07	$8,003.10	$5,149.78	$2,485.70	$0.00
5.0 yrs	$30,000.00	$12,699.35	$9,143.20	$5,852.78	$2,810.56	$0.00
Cash Flow	$1,300,000.00	$60,183.21	$43,916.38	$28,491.62	$13,866.37	$0.00
True Yield	6.00 %	6.25 %	6.00 %	5.76 %	5.54 %	5.32 %
Variance		$16,266.83	$0.00	$(15,424.75)	$(30,050.00)	$(43,916.38)

Let's assume the public fund has a $1 million portfolio. The money is invested in a single bond purchased at par at a purchase yield of 6 percent for five years. The purchase yield of the portfolio is used to estimate the amount of money the public fund can budget. We assume for purposes of illustration that 6 percent of $1 million ($60,000) is the annual budget for each of the next five years. This means no cash flow from coupons will be invested; all will be spent as received. In the absence of reinvested coupons, the fund forgoes "interest on interest" to the tune of $43,916.38 over the five-year life of the bond, reducing the true yield to 5.32 percent, not 6 percent, as Wall Street would report it. Thus the fund's return is not really a yield to maturity but a simple yield.

If you apply the reinvestment assumption to a $100 million or $1 billion portfolio, you have a huge overstatement of fund performance whenever coupons are spent. The alternative is to use total return to report portfolio performance, confirming this book's earlier point that total return provides little relevance when reconciling budget forecasting with portfolio performance measurement.

In this chapter we've tackled part of the price volatility problem. You now have a tool to help you tame the dragon of price volatility, at least for noncallable securities. But fortunately, noncallables are not the only investments at the fund manager's disposal. We turn to *callable securities* next.

POINTS TO REMEMBER

- Duration is a much better tool than average life for assessing the price volatility of a bond or bond portfolio.
- Modified duration applies to noncallable bonds.
- Effective duration applies to callable bonds and other securities whose cash flows may change.
- Yield to maturity contains a reinvestment assumption that does not hold when public funds spend coupons as they are received. Consequently, the actual returns are lower.

CHAPTER 9

Callable Securities

Risk is the only certainty—change the only constant.

—GREGORY J. MILLMAN, *THE VANDALS' CROWN*

KEY POINTS COVERED IN THIS CHAPTER

- The anatomy of U.S. Agency callable securities
- Using Bloomberg to access the features of callable agencies
- How to assess value in callable securities
- Bullets versus callables

Callable securities are an asset class that public fund managers can use to pursue their goals of safety, liquidity, and income. The universe of callable securities is broad, involving a host of issuers, sectors and structures—too broad to cover within the scope of this chapter. Thus we have limited our coverage of callables to those issued by U.S. Agencies. Mortgage-backed securities (MBSs), collateralized mortgage obligations (CMOs), and other securitized single, multifamily, and commercial loans are among the excluded. Those securities are described in other texts, the most complete being Frank J. Fabozzi's *The Handbook of Fixed Income Securities.*[1] While this chapter highlights callable agencies, the reader should *not* infer that we advocate them over bullets, corporates, MBSs, or any other securities.

Within the universe of U.S. Agencies (hereafter, simply agencies), we will address securities structured as fixed, step-up continuous, discrete, one-time, and canary. If these terms are puzzling, don't worry; they will be explained in due course. Our goal here to provide readers with a general understanding of callable agencies and with commonsense tools for determining their value and their suitability as portfolio assets from a Main Street perspective. These securities present public funds managers with unique challenges regarding the imperatives of investment policy—namely, to assure safety of principal, liquidity, and a market rate of return.

As we begin, we need to remind ourselves of two facts of life in the public fund business. First, as we have emphasized throughout this book, risk for public fund managers is asymmetrical. A dollar of pain or loss carries more weight than a dollar of gain. Consequently, managers must focus their investment strategies on producing returns consistent with stable budgets, and eschew Wall Street's preoccupation with total returns. Second, not all securities are created politically and economically equal. Some have credit, interest-rate, and reinvestment risks that offer more or less value relative to Main Street than to Wall Street.

We should also remind ourselves fund managers are obliged to preserve principal even as they pursue investment income consistent with policy objectives of safety, liquidity, and income. So should managers adopt a buy-and-hold style? Should they be active traders? We recommend neither. Instead, we are proponents of passive management, and shun both buy-and-hold and active management investment styles as being contrary to the normal operations and financial stewardship required by most public funds. This is not to say that valid exceptions for both do not exist; however, passive management is the most consistent link between investment practice and the implicit and explicit objectives of investment policy. In this sense, the ways of Wall Street must be modified to the needs of Main Street.

THE ANATOMY OF U.S. AGENCY CALLABLE BONDS

Several agencies of the federal government sell their debt to the public. From the investor's perspective, these securities have a number of attractive features: They maintain the implicit backing of the federal government, many have good marketability, and all offer a slightly higher yield than do U.S. Treasury securities of equal maturities. Those yield differences, as of spring 2005, are shown in Exhibit 9-1. As we'll see later, callable agency issues offer still higher yields to investors. The higher yields of callable agencies are designed to compensate investors so their securities can be redeemed at the convenience of the issuer.

EXHIBIT 9-1
TREASURY VERSUS BULLET AGENCY YIELDS

	Maturity			
	2-Year	**3-Year**	**4-Year**	**5-Year**
Treasury	2.58	3.18	3.61	3.93
Bullet Agency	2.93	3.57	4.04	4.50

Callable bonds have several elements you must understand before you consider them for your portfolio: fixed versus step-up coupons, call structures, and lockouts.

Fixed Versus Step-Up Coupons

In this chapter we refer to two coupon arrangements: fixed and step-up. A fixed coupon is exactly what you'd think: the coupon remains the same over the life of the bond. A bond with a *step-up coupon,* on the other hand, is one whose coupon increases incrementally over the life of the security. The *canary* bond is unique in that it is callable during the period before the security converts to a noncallable or bullet structure; the canary callable coupon can possess a step-up feature. During the call period before conversion and/or at conversion the canary can be structured to have its coupon step up. The lockout refers to the period before the canary converts from a callable bond to a bullet. The amount of coupon step-up and the frequency of the step-up vary from issue to issue for both step-ups and canarys.

Call Structures

Call structures take three basic forms: continuous (or American), one-time (European), and discrete (Bermuda). *Continuous* structure is analogous to the U.S. option market, which allows the buyer of an option to exercise that option any time prior to the expiration—hence the term "American." In the callable bond world, however, the option remains with the issuer, who has the right (but not the obligation) to redeem a security at any time—that is, continuously—prior to maturity.

European structure reflects the option market throughout Europe, where the option holder can only exercise the option at expiration. A bond that carries this European structure gives the issuer the right (but not the obligation) to call the bond on one specified date. In most cases, we refer to these as *one-time* or *1-X* callable bonds.

Bermuda structure reflects the middle ground between American and European, hence the term Bermuda, which is located geographically between the two continents (Exhibit 9-2). They are also called *discrete* because their optionality is neither continuous nor one-time, but usually callable quarterly or on semi-annual coupon dates up to maturity. The canary described earlier likewise derives its name from geography; the Canary Islands are located between Europe and both Bermuda and America.

Lockout

Whether they adopt the continuous, one-time, or discrete structure, all callable securities have some period of call protection, usually referred to

EXHIBIT 9-2

THE GEOGRAPHY OF AMERICAN, BERMUDA, AND EUROPEAN CALL STRUCTURES

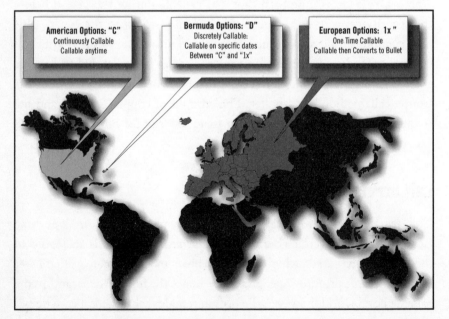

American Options: "C"
Continuously Callable
Callable anytime

Bermuda Options: "D"
Discretely Callable:
Callable on specific dates
Between "C" and "1x"

European Options: 1x "
One Time Callable
Callable then Converts to Bullet

as the *lockout period*. This is the time period during which the coupon is assured to the bondholder—the time before the issuer has the right to exercise his option to call the bond. Depending on the callable security's maturity, this period of call protection usually ranges from one month to five years. Once the lockout period has expired, the issuer can call the security. For example, for a continuously callable agency with a three-year maturity and a three-month lockout period, the issuer can redeem the security at any time between the end of the three-month lockout and maturity. Issuers typically provide notice of redemption five business days prior to the actual call.

USING BLOOMBERG TO OBTAIN AGENCY INFORMATION

Fund managers can find listings for most newly issued agency securities and obtain the details of their coupons, maturities, underwriters, and call features by going to Bloomberg's New Issue Monitor (NIM) page (Exhibit

EXHIBIT 9-3
BLOOMBERG NEW ISSUE MONITOR (NIM)

```
NIM                                              N236 Govt   NIM
Enter # <GO> for a standard or custom selection
                    NEW ISSUE MONITOR
                       Standard Selections
   1) U.S. Bond Market              9) Japanese Domestic Market
   2) U.S. Agencies               10) Price Talk/Expected Issues
   3) U.S. Corporates/144A/PrivPlcmt  11) Asia Ex-Japan
   4) Eurobond Market             12) Canadian Domestic Market
   5) Equity-Linked Securities    13) Europe/Asia/Africa Loans
   6) Preferred Market            14) North/South America Loans
   7) Euro Zone Market            15) Latin America
   8) U.S. MTN/BKNT/DPNT/CD        16) All Issues
                        Custom Selections
  31) Create Selection            36) Create Selection
  32) Create Selection            37) Create Selection
  33) Create Selection            38) Create Selection
  34) Create Selection            39) Create Selection
  35) Create Selection            40) Create Selection
                       Related Calendars
  41) MCAL Structured Finance     44) CDRN Municipal Negotiated
  42) CDRC Municipal Competitive  45) ECDR Equity
  43) ROAD Bloomberg Road Shows   46) LEAG Bloomberg Underwriter Rankings
          99 <GO> for New Issues contact information

Australia 61 2 9777 8600      Brazil 5511 3048 4500      Europe 44 20 7330 7500      Germany 49 69 920410
Hong Kong 852 2977 6000 Japan 81 3 3201 8900 Singapore 65 6212 1000 U.S. 1 212 318 2000 Copyright 2005 Bloomberg L.P.
                                                              G457-32-1 08-Apr-05 5:40:59
```

9-3) and entering "2," for U.S. Agencies. Managers who lack Bloomberg access can simply request these details from their broker or investment advisor.

Entering 2 takes you to the U.S. Agencies screen. Exhibit 9-4 is a typical Bloomberg NIM2 page. Bloomberg's shorthand for describing an agency callable bond (shown in the right-most column) is to put the term of the bond maturity first, separated by a hyphen and the letters NC (for noncallable) followed by the lockout period—for example, 3MO (for 3 months) or 1 (for 1 year). The abbreviation CONT, for continuous, may follow as well. A 3-year continuously callable agency with a three-month lockout would be described as 3-NC3MO CONT.

Bonds with American (Continuous) Call Options

To get a better feel for Bloomberg online data, let's see how it describes an agency with a continuous call feature. Look at line 10 on the Bloomberg

EXHIBIT 9-4
BLOOMBERG NIM2 PAGE

```
Page                                        N236 Govt   NIM

New Issues: Agencies                        Phone: 646-834-7320
                   Cpn    Mty     Sprd  Outstand  Book Mgr
    Issuer         (%)   (M/D/Y)  (BP)  Amt (Mil) (*=group)  Note
 1) FED HOME LN BANK STEP  04/29/10       USD 50   JPM,RBCDR  5-NC3MO   INC
 2) FED FARM CREDIT  4.7   10/06/08       USD 35   HSBC       3.5-NC1 CONT
 3) FED FARM CREDIT  4.1   04/11/07       USD 50   UBS        2-NC
 4) FED FARM CREDIT  5.61  04/06/20       USD 50   DB,RBCDR   15-NC5   CONT
 5) FED HOME LN BANK 4     10/27/06       USD 15   MK         1.5-NC1    1X
 6) FANNIE MAE       STEP  04/25/08       USD 25   FTN        3-NC1    RETL
 7) FED HOME LN BANK 4.05  10/27/06       USD 25   BAS        1.5-NC1MO
 8) FED FARM CREDIT  4¼    12/06/07       USD 20   WFC        2.75-NC
 9) FED HOME LN BANK 5⅜    04/22/15       USD 5    JPM        10-NC5   CONT
10) FED HOME LN BANK 4.65  04/15/08       USD 15   WFC        3-NC3MO  CONT
11) FED HOME LN BANK 6     04/27/22       USD 25   ADV,SUN    17-NC2   CONT
12) FED HOME LN BANK 5     10/14/09       USD 20   CW,WFC     4.5-NC6MO
13) FANNIE MAE       4.31  04/20/07       USD 50   BAS,FTN    2-NC3MO  BERM
14) FED HOME LN BANK 5.05  10/21/09       USD 25   WFC        4.5-NC3MO
15) FED HOME LN BANK 4.01  10/27/06       USD 15   MK         1.5-NC1    1X
16) FED HOME LN BANK 4.01  10/27/06       USD 50   JEFF,SUN   2½-NC6M  INC
                  -------- TUESDAY, MARCH 29 --------
17) FED HOME LN BANK STEP  05/18/06       USD 25   SIEBRT     1-NC3MO
18) FED HOME LN BANK 5¼    04/28/08       USD 25   VS         3-NC1     INC
19) FED HOME LN BANK 6.2   04/20/20       USD 100  GS,ML      15-NC3MO
Australia 61 2 9777 8600    Brazil 5511 3048 4500   Europe 44 20 7330 7500   Germany 49 69 920410
Hong Kong 852 2977 6000 Japan 81 3 3201 8900 Singapore 65 6212 1000 U.S. 1 212 318 2000 Copyright 2005 Bloomberg L.P.
                                                              G457-32-2 08-Apr-05  5:46:19
```

NIM2 page in Exhibit 9-4. Reading left to right: we see the issuer of this security is the Federal Home Loan Bank (FED HOME LN BANK). The bond has a 4.65 percent coupon maturing on 04/15/08 (April 15, 2008), and the issue size is $15 million. The underwriter in this case is WFC (Wells Fargo). The "Note" column tells us other critical information: 3-NC3MO CONT. This shorthand means the bond is a 3-year agency and is not callable (NC) for the first three months after issue, but is continuously callable thereafter. Given the maturity date and the fact that it is a 3-year security, we know the issue date is April 15, 2005. So the lockout period begins then. Anyone interested in purchasing this issue would commit to doing so on March 30, 2005 (the trade date). Settlement would take place (typically delivery versus payment, or DVP) on April 15, 2005.

Bonds with Bermuda Call Options

We stated earlier Bermuda-type callable bonds are callable only on specific dates, typically, quarterly or semi-annually. One of these Bermuda bonds can be seen in Exhibit 9-4 on line 13. Again, reading left to right, we see this bond was issued by FANNIE MAE with a 4.31 percent coupon and maturity date of April 20, 2007. The issue size is $50 million, and the underwriters are BAS (Bank of America Securities) and FTN (First Tennessee). The right-most column contains the information we seek about call features: 2-NC3MO BERM. This tells us the 2-year Bermuda bond is not callable (NC) during the first three months after issue. Being a Bermuda type, it is callable only quarterly once the three-month lockout period has expired. The issuer, in essence, has four dates each year to call the security. Bermuda type bonds can also be structured to be callable on their semi-annual coupon dates after the initial lockout period. How can you know the quarterly or semi-annual dates apply? This and other important information about a particular bond can be accessed by clicking on the bond of interest on the Bloomberg screen.

European Option Callables

European type callable bonds, frequently referred to as *one-time* or *1-X*, have, as the name implies, a single call date. If the issuer chooses *not* to call on that date, the bond converts, in effect, to a bullet (not callable) for its remaining maturity.

An agency of this type is found on line 5 of the NIM2 screen shown in Exhibit 9-4. Again reading left to right; we see the Federal Home Loan Bank (FED HOME LN BANK) has issued a 4 percent bond maturing on October 27, 2006. The notation 1.5-NC1 1X indicates the 1.5-year (18-month) issue is call protected for one year from the issue date, at which point the issuer must decide whether to exercise its option to call the issue. If the option is not exercised, the issue converts to a bullet for the remaining six months of its life.

Step-Up Bonds

You recall a step-up callable agency is one whose coupons increase incrementally over the life of the bond. One of these step-up bonds appears on line 12 of the next NIM screen, Exhibit 9-5. Here we have a Freddie Mac issue. But notice the word STEP is in the column where the coupon information should be. This indicates the issue will have multiple coupons. The rest of the information is straightforward. The issue size is $25 million and is offered by UBS (Union Bank of Switzerland). The shorthand in the right-most column—5-NC6MO—means it has a 5-year maturity with six months of call protection. After that six-month lockout, the security is callable semi-annually, on coupon payment dates.

You're probably asking yourself, "What is the coupon rate, and how and when does it step up?" Again, clicking on the bond of interest will take you to another Bloomberg page, where these important details are listed. If you did buy this particular bond, you'd find the initial coupon is 4.10 percent. If the bond is not called by October 5, 2005 the coupon will step up to 5.00 percent and remains at that level until October 5, 2006. If the security has not been called on or before October 5, 2006, the coupon will step up once again. The next step up is 50 basis points, moving the coupon to 5.50 percent. The 5.50 percent coupon remains for the life of the security.

Canary Callables

A canary callable is a bond that is discretely callable for some initial time period and then converts to a bullet. Canary callables can have fixed

EXHIBIT 9-5
MORE ON BLOOMBERG NIM2 PAGE

```
Menu                                              N236 Govt   NIM
Enter # <GO> for DES.                                    Page 13 / 23
New Issues: Agencies                              Phone: 646-834-7320
                    Cpn     Mty     Sprd  Outstand   Book Mgr
     Issuer         (%)   (M/D/Y)   (BP)  Amt (Mil)  (*=group)   Note
 1) FED HOME LN BANK STEP   04/21/06       USD 25    LEGG        1-NC3MO
 2) FED HOME LN BANK 4½     03/30/09       USD 200   UBS         4-NC
 3) FED HOME LN BANK 4.01   10/20/06       USD 30    ADV,SUN     1.5-NC6MO 1X
 4) Fannie Mae Announces $3 Bln Sale 10-Year Benchmark Notes; Pricing March 29
 5) FED HOME LN BANK 4.65   04/21/08       USD 50    WFC         3-NC1    CONT
 6) FED HOME LN BANK 5      04/20/10       USD 40    FTN         5-NC2    CONT
 7) FED HOME LN BANK STEP   04/22/10       USD 25    MK,VS       5-NC3MO CNRY
 8) FED HOME LN BANK 5¾     04/20/10       USD 15    FTN         5-NC2       1X
 9) FANNIE MAE       4.45   10/12/07       USD 100   BCLY        2.5-NC6M  1X
10) FED HOME LN BANK 3.71   04/13/06       USD 25    GKST        1-NC
11) FREDDIE MAC      STEP   04/03/20       USD 25    ML          15-NC1
12) FREDDIE MAC      STEP   04/05/10       USD 25    UBS         5-NC6MO
13) FED HOME LN BANK 4.28   04/20/07       USD 25    FTN         2-NC3MO
14) FED HOME LN BANK 4.08   12/29/06       USD 15    MK          1.75-NC1  1X
15) FED HOME LN BANK 5¼     04/22/10       USD 25    MK,RBCDR    5-NC3MO
16) FED HOME LN BANK 4¼     04/18/07       USD 35    MK,RBCDR    2-NC1     1X
17) FED HOME LN BANK 4½     10/19/07       USD 15    ML          2.5-NC6MO
18) FED HOME LN BANK 5      04/21/10       USD 25    SUN         5-NC1     1X
19) FED HOME LN BANK 5.17   04/21/10       USD 15    INCAP       5-NC6MO
20) FANNIE MAE       5      04/06/10       USD 300   JOINT LEADS 5-NC1     1X
Australia 61 2 9777 8600      Brazil 5511 3048 4500    Europe 44 20 7330 7500      Germany 49 69 920410
Hong Kong 852 2977 6000 Japan 81 3 3201 8900 Singapore 65 6212 1000 U.S. 1 212 318 2000 Copyright 2005 Bloomberg L.P.
                                                             G457-32-0 10-Apr-05 11:30:53
```

coupons or coupons that step up. For example, a 5-year non-call 2-year (5nc2 in market parlance) canary callable indicates a bond that is discretely callable (usually every six months) for the first two years and then converts, if not called, to a 3-year bullet.

We find a canary issued by the Federal Home Loan Bank on line 7 of the Bloomberg NIM2 page shown in Exhibit 9-5. Again, where we would normally see the coupon rate, we find the word STEP. This $25 million new issue, which matures on April 22, 2010, is offered by MK (Morgan Keegan) and VS (Vining Sparks). The right-most column indicates the following: 5-NC3MO CNRY. We conclude it is a 5-year bond, with a 3-month lockout during which it cannot be called. The CNRY designation indicates a canary, meaning it will convert to noncallable status after the call period. We can learn on another screen that the initial coupon is 4 percent. After the lockout the security is callable quarterly until April 22, 2006. On that date the issuer must decide whether to call and redeem the security. If the issuer does not redeem or call the bond two things happen: first, the coupon steps up from 4 percent to 6 percent; second, the bond will convert from a callable to a bullet for the remaining four years. Again, clicking through will take you to a Bloomberg page containing the important details not shown in the NIM2 page.

UNDERSTANDING VALUE AND RISK IN CALLABLE SECURITIES

All investors are concerned with two things: value and risk. Whether we are investing in financial assets such as stocks and bonds, or real assets such as office buildings, these two things are never far from their minds. We ask ourselves, "What is this thing worth?" and "What are the risks involved in owning it?" Every public fund investor asks the same two questions, which are very much related since risk has a very real impact on value. We delve into these questions here because value and risk have a political dimension that must be accounted for in portfolio decisions.

First, what is value? Conceptually, the value of all financial and real assets is a function of cash flows. The bond investor, for example, receives cash flows in the form of coupons and a return of principal at redemption. Even a piece of undeveloped land has cash flows: outgoing negative flows in the form of annual property tax payments, and one big positive inflow when the land is sold.

Value is assessed in terms of the

- amount of cash flows
- timing of cash flows
- certainty or uncertainty of those cash flows.

For example, we put a higher value on an investment producing a stream of cash flows coming to us shortly after we invest—and in larger amounts— than another investment that produces cash flows in smaller amounts and for which we must wait a long, long time. And, if the timing and amount of cash flows are the same, we place a higher value on the investment with more certain, less risky cash flows. Thus, value differences between securities are derived from market forces that may interrupt—either temporarily or permanently—the expected amount, timing, and certainty of cash flows due us, the investors.

These observations about value should be universal, applying to Wall Street and Main Street in equal measure. However, the political realities of Main Street require a slightly different view of value. Both Main and Wall Streets equate market price with value. This makes sense because the market price of a bond reflects the bond's stream of cash flows *and* the risks surrounding those cash flows. But Main Street investors must also consider the volatility of market price during the holding period of the bond. Price volatility during that period can produce GASB 31–related political problems for the fund, as noted in earlier chapters. It can also produce risk to principal in the event that the bond must be liquidated prior to maturity.

Even so-called risk-free U.S. Treasuries are evaluated with the timing, amounts, and certainty of cash flows in mind. "But there is no uncertainty in these," one might argue. "The U.S. government will always make good on its interest and principal repayments." True, but if unforeseen circumstances force a fund manager to liquidate a T-note prior to maturity—when the market price is down—the value of the cash flows from that investment will not be what the manager had anticipated. Thus, price and value are not necessarily the same from the perspective of Main Street. Academia's axiom that U.S. Treasury debt represents the risk-free "rate" of interest, though correct, obscures this reality, causing many investors to believe Treasuries are risk-free, which is not the case. Treasury debt is risk-free from the perspective of creditworthiness, and only if it is held to maturity. Main Street investors, who face liquidity needs, cannot always assume their assets will be held to maturity.

As in other aspects of public fund investing, the ways of Wall Street must be modified to meet the needs of Main Street. Unlike his Wall Street cousins, the Main Street investor cannot limit his concerns to economic risk and trade-offs when making decisions about the value of securities. He must also consider political risks. Insofar as callable securities are concerned, this means the Main Street investor must recognize the three primary risks—interest-rate risk, credit risk, and reinvestment risk—do not carry the same political or economic weights. For example, interest-rate risk threatens principal (political), while reinvestment risk threatens fund income (primarily economic). On the strictly economic front, the investor must also appraise the trade-off between the higher yield of the callable and the certainty of cash flows given up to obtain it. Is that yield high enough to compensate the fund when the issuer can call the bond away at its convenience?

When considering callable agency securities, public fund managers must prioritize the three risks—reinvestment risk, credit risk, and interest-rate risk—in terms of both economics and politics. Here is our assessment of risk, from lowest to highest.

Reinvestment risk, the risk of having to reinvest principal at a lower rate, is the next lowest in our pecking order of political risk. **Reinvestment risk is not an issue of principal loss but of income loss.** It affects the politics of budgeting, but not the politics of financial reporting, which can be deadly. Ever since the Orange County debacle and the GASB 31 requirements that followed in its wake, financial reporting has been a significant political risk for the stewards of public funds.

While some readers might take issue with our weighting of these risks, prioritizing them is essential. In our case, we believe credit risk is the *least* politically perilous of the three (albeit at this writing there is pressure on Congress to remove the government-sponsored enterprise [GSE] status of bond-issuing agencies). The low probability of a federal agency defaulting on interest payments or principal repayments is the primary reason we classify it as the lowest political risk.

Interest-rate risk represents the greatest political risk, because of both the potential necessity to report GASB 31 unrealized losses, and the possibility of causing real losses to principal if the fund must liquidate securities before maturity at a price below the initial purchase price.

Example of Main Street Analysis

Let's illustrate how the prioritizing of risk can guide decision making in the real world of public fund strategy. For simplicity we will keep the discussion on the level of the individual security, not at the portfolio level, as in this example:

The City of Janeville is considering two alternative investments: a non-callable 3-year U.S. Treasury note (USTN) yielding 3.79 percent versus a 3-year Federal Home Loan Bank (FHLB) with a 4.32 percent yield. This callable agency has a Bermuda option with a one-year lockout period.

Remember a Bermuda, or discrete, bond is callable only on coupon dates up to maturity. So here we go, beginning with risk assessment:

Callable versus Noncallable Risk Assessment

	USTN	FHLB
	3-year, 3.79 percent yield	3-year, 4.32 percent yield
	Noncallable	Callable; 1-year lockout Bermuda
Credit risk	None. Backed by full faith and credit of the U.S. government	Greater, but with implicit backing of U.S. government Rated AAA
Interest-rate risk	Greater. 2.67 duration	Lower. 1.96 duration
Reinvestment risk	None. Noncallable	Greater. Can be called four times between lockout and maturity
Income	Less income	Greater Income

So, when we assess the pros and cons of these two very different securities, we can make the following summary statements:

U.S. T-Note (USTN)

- Pros: Absolutely default-free. Income is certain because the T-note cannot be called away; consequently, the note presents no reinvestment risk during its life.
- Cons: Not so good for the budget because it offers less income. Also, the higher duration subjects the fund to greater price volatility (GASB 31 exposure) than the agency.

FHLB Agency

- Pros: Higher income. Lower duration means less price volatility (GASB 31 exposure).

- Cons: Higher reinvestment risk because it can be called after the one-year lockout.

So we have a mixed bag. Each of the securities has valuable qualities, but each also has negatives. How can we sort these out? Perhaps the best way is to frame the final evaluation in terms of three possible market scenarios, one of which will prevail:

Scenario 1. Rates remain unchanged
Scenario 2. Rates rise: yields go up; bond prices go down
Scenario 3. Rates fall: yield goes down; bond prices rise

Budgets and GASB 31 reporting are typically done on a 12-month basis. While budgets are based on either calendar or fiscal year reporting periods, evaluations should focus on rolling 12-month periods. That being said, let's look at the three possible scenarios, a framework for evaluating our choices.

Scenario 1. Rates remain unchanged The callable agency has at least one year of call protection, implying an 18 percent budget advantage (53 basis points) over the USTN during that period. For a $100 million portfolio, the difference is $530,000 per year. In this rate environment, substituting a slight credit and reinvestment risk for the full faith and credit of the USTN over the next 12 months seems reasonable—$530,000 can purchase lots of goods and services.

Scenario 2. Rates rise: yields go up; bond prices go down. Depending on the magnitude of the rate increase, both securities will produce GASB 31 reporting losses. If the market rate rise is 100 basis points or less, the recognized but unrealized loss on the callable agency will be less than that of the USTN because its beginning duration is substantially lower: 1.96 versus 2.67, or 26 percent less initial interest-rate risk.

Assuming the public fund will not sell its securities at losses, the callable agency provides substantially more income. If rates remain high, then the likelihood of the agency being called is remote. Again, the budget is the beneficiary.

More important, the price volatility of the agency will be less than the USTN by virtue of its lower duration, meaning lower price risk (i.e., political risk). **Politically, the trade-off should always favor principal certainty over income certainty.**

Scenario 3. Rates fall: yields go down; bond prices rise. The USTN shines brightest in this scenario. For the agency holder, on the other hand, the outlook is disconcerting—assuming the one-year lockout period has expired. A rate drop as small as 25 basis points could induce the issuing agency to call its security, forcing the fund to reinvest the redeemed principal at a lower rate. There are two other consequences to consider:

- The loss of revenue caused by reinvestment at a lower rate means the break-even rate has to be at least 25 basis points lower since the callable provided a 50 basis point advantage for the first year.
- It must be assumed in reinvesting the callable redemption proceeds that the fund manager will not find a duration-matched callable equal to or above the reinvestment rate needed to equal that of the USTN.

So we have examined three scenarios and their outcomes. The fund manager must decide which of these outcomes is most likely and which trade-off is most sensible. Remember, though, our example is based on individual securities, not on the portfolio as a whole. No portfolio should consist entirely of bullets or callables; rather, there should be a balance of the two. Where that balance should be depends on the fund's priorities with respect to politics, the budget, and the organization's portfolio management expertise.

WHICH STRUCTURE OFFERS THE BEST VALUE?

When Wall Street money managers assess value, they have a strong focus on marketability, where marketability is defined as the lowest transaction cost (bid/offer spread). High transaction costs are performance killers. Wall Street money managers are active traders who justify their existence by beating on a total return basis at a predetermined market index. Their performance will usually be as volatile as the market they are indexing. Main Street fund managers, in contrast, tend to focus less on marketability and more on cash management, cash flow certainty, income, and then marketability. Let's consider each.

Cash Management

The structure of a callable is more or less important depending on its role in the portfolio. Recall our recommendation in an earlier chapter in which managers earmark some assets for primary liquidity and others for secondary (or backup) liquidity. Callables are most valuable in the secondary liquidity or income role. As long as maturities are short and primary liquidity needs are already met, callables are useful instruments of cash management and help enhance the portfolio return. Again, fund managers must decide whether the greater return of callables warrants the added cash flow uncertainty associated with them.

Cash Flow Certainty

Here the investor considers certainty as it relates to the amount and timing of future cash flows. A continuous structure is by far the *least* certain in that it gives so many call opportunities to the issuer. Theoretically, a continuous security can be called away at any moment beyond the lockout period, forcing the manager to reinvest at a different rate. And who can know in advance what that rate will be, and what cash flows will follow? So the question for the fund manager is this: Does the additional yield of a particular call structure—such as continuous—fully compensate the investor for the uncertainty it creates? In our view, continuously callable bonds rarely do. Thus, we would favor discrete and one-time call structures.

Income

Greater risk translates into greater return, at least in theory. The continuous call structure clearly has the greatest reinvestment risk and should offer the greater return. For the investor, the question again is whether that incrementally higher yield compensates for the greater risk.

Marketability

In terms of marketability, the investor must consider the bid/offer spread he or she will face should it be necessary to liquidate the security to meet a fiscal obligation or rebalance the portfolio. Large spreads diminish value. For the typical public fund, the best marketability is found in callables with one-time and discrete structures.

Exhibit 9-6 summarizes the value difference of callable structures relative to income, cash flow certainty, marketability, and cash management. You can use this exhibit in helping to analyze investment choices.

EXHIBIT 9-6
VALUE DIFFERENCES OF CALLABLE STRUCTURES ON FOUR KEY DIMENSIONS

	Cash Management	Cash Flow Certainty	Income	Marketability
Continuous	Weakest	Lowest	Highest	Lowest
Discrete	Moderate	Low	High	Low
One-Time	Strongest	Highest	Lowest	High

WHICH OPTION OFFERS THE BEST RELATIVE VALUE?

In purchasing a callable security, a fund manager, in effect, grants an option to the issuer—the option to call or not call the security at some time prior to maturity. In the Iron Laws of Finance, every option has a value—and some options have more value than others. Because an option has value, the fund manager should receive something in return. That "something" is a higher return than is available from equivalent *noncallable* securities. But how can we know if we have made a good trade? A good way is to assess what was given up for the higher return. Consider this example:

> Tim has purchased an agency with a continuous callable structure. In other words, Tim has given the issuer the right to take away his security on any day between the end of the lockout period and maturity. How many days are those—a hundred, a thousand? The more days, the more that has been given away. Had he purchased an agency with a one-time call option, in comparison, Tim would have given away much less.

Once you start thinking about the value of the option demanded by the issuer, and the yield received in return, you can make some judgments about the merits of the investment from the fund's perspective.

The option table shown in Exhibit 9-7 underscores the value disparity between the various callable structures. The quantities indicated in the exhibit are the number of options given to the issuer. For example, consider the 5-year, continuous callable security with the three-month lockout. In purchasing that security, you will have given the issuer 1,197 opportunities to call away your investment. Does the higher yield of this security provide adequate compensation to the investor for this arrangement? We have rarely seen agency yields that justify this trade-off. The 5-year discretely callable, possessing the same three-month lockout period, in contrast, gives the issuer only 19 opportunities to exercise a call. From the investor's perspective, this trade-off is clearly more appealing in terms of cash management, cash flow certainty, and marketability. The only question is: How much less yield must you accept in return?

EXHIBIT 9-7
NUMBER OF OPTIONS SOLD TO MATURITY

Call Structure	Lockout		
	3-Month	6-Month	1-Year
2-Year One-Time	1	1	1
2-Year Discrete	7	3	2
2-Year Continuous	441	378	252
3-Year One-Time	1	1	1
3-Year Discrete	11	5	4
3-Year Continuous	693	630	504
4-Year One-Time	1	1	1
4-Year Discrete	15	7	6
4-Year Continuous	945	882	756
5-Year One-Time	1	1	1
5-Year Discrete	19	9	8
5-Year Continuous	1197	1134	1008

Another way to assess the trade-off made by investors in purchasing callables is to examine the yield spread between securities with various call options. We've calculated a number of these in Exhibit 9-8. To understand this exhibit, ask yourself the following question: Do you have any idea what yield advantage you would receive if you purchased a 2-year continuous callable with a three-month lockout instead of a 2-year discrete callable with the same lockout period? The second line shows only 1 basis point difference in the yields of these two securities—and in favor of the continuous callable. Furthermore, the investor gains 5 extra basis points (five one-hundredths of one percent) when the choice is between the same securities with 5-year maturities. You have to ask yourself, "Is this a fair trade? Is the pickup in yield worth the additional options given to the issuer?" If current income is the number one portfolio priority, the discretely callable option structure appears to offer the best value, where value is defined as a balance between call options sold and the coupon received. For a bond with a 5-year maturity and a 3-month lockout, the owner of the continuous version is paid only 5 basis points (five one-hundredths of 1 percent) more than the owner of the discretely callable security with the same maturity and lockout period. This is in spite of the fact that the issuer of the continuous security has 1,178 more opportunities to call it its option (1,197 minus 19 call dates = 1,178 per Exhibit 9-7). This, in our view, is not a good risk/return trade-off.

In our opinion, neither 1 nor 5 basis points provides sufficient benefit to income to compensate the fund for the fact that the continuous call feature gives the issuer many opportunities to improve its own financial situation to the detriment of the investor's. The reader may reach a different conclusion.

EXHIBIT 9-8
BASIS POINT SPREAD FOR VARIOUS CALL STRUCTURES

	Lockout Period		
	3-Month	6-Month	1-Year
2-year discrete vs. 2-year 1-X	5	0	0
2-year continuous vs. 2-year discrete	1	0	0
3-year discrete vs. 3-year 1-X	8	1	0
3-year continuous vs. 3-year discrete	2	0	0
4-year discrete vs. 4-year 1-X	15	8	1
4-year continuous vs. 4-year discrete	4	3	0
5-year discrete vs. 5-year 1-X	19	12	6
5-year continuous vs. 5-year discrete	5	4	3

One striking conclusion emerges from our discussion and the exhibits to this point: the lack of value found in continuously callable structures. In trying to balance the value of certainty versus uncertainty, there is little reason to ever choose a continuous structure. If current income is the number one portfolio priority, the discretely callable option structure appears to offer the best value, where value is defined as a balance between call options sold and the coupon received.

LOCKOUTS AND VALUE

Another way to assess the value of different call structures is to consider the lockout period. We've defined the lockout period as the period of time subsequent to issue during which a security cannot be called. All call structures include a shorter or longer lockout period. A shorter lockout period benefits the issuer exclusively. If market rates drop, the issuer can quickly call and redeem outstanding bonds and sell new ones at lower rates, saving millions in interest expenses. But what's good for the issuer in that instance is bad for the investor, who would have her security called away. Intuitively, we know a shorter lockout period should be compensated through the coupon yield because it's disadvantageous for the investor. But are investors, in fact, adequately compensated? Is the compensation for a short lockout period significantly higher than for a longer period? Exhibit 9-9 quantifies the investor's yield pickup for various lockouts and structures as of May 2005. The exhibit quantifies the very small yield differences between short and long lockout periods. For example, the 3-year one-time callable with a three-month lockout provides only 9 basis points (380 minus 371) greater yield than the same security with one year of call protection. The fund managers must ask, "Is this extra yield worth the call option I'd be giving the issuer?"

TREASURY BULLETS VERSUS CALLABLES AGENCIES

Every public fund manager must regularly choose between bullet Treasuries and callable securities. Each has something to offer, so which should the manager choose? As the following discussion will indicate, there is no clear answer. Each should play a role in the manager's portfolio. The problem comes when managers use all of one or all of the other exclusively.

EXHIBIT 9-9
PERCENT YIELD SPREADS BETWEEN DIFFERENT LOCKOUT PERIODS

	Lockout		
Structure	3-Month	6-Month	1-Year
2-Year One-Time	3.08	3.07	3.00
2-Year Discrete	3.13	3.07	3.00
2-Year Continuous	3.14	3.07	3.00
3-Year One-Time	3.80	3.77	3.71
3-Year Discrete	3.88	3.78	3.71
3-Year Continuous	3.90	3.78	3.71
4-Year One-Time	4.31	4.28	4.23
4-Year Discrete	4.46	4.36	4.24
4-Year Continuous	4.50	4.39	4.25
5-Year One-Time	4.68	4.66	4.62
5-Year Discrete	4.87	4.78	4.68
5-Year Continuous	4.92	4.82	4.71

Let's review the risks and rewards of each of these investment securities. To make this easier to follow, we have summarized this information in table form in Exhibit 9-10.

Note: The following table summarizes the risk/return characteristics of a 3-year maturity-matched USTN to a 3-year non-callable 3-month U.S. Agency discretely callable.

EXHIBIT 9-10
RISK/RETURN OVERVIEW

Risk Type	Bullet Treasury	Callable Agency
Interest-rate risk (duration)	• More interest-rate risk because of longer duration • More political risk due to price volatility	• Less interest-rate risk because of shorter duration • Higher coupon, more income
Reinvestment risk (yield)	• Less reinvestment risk • Certain cash flows • Lower income but better cash management	• Higher reinvestment risk • More uncertain cash flows • Higher yield
Credit risk (yield)	• Full faith & credit of the federal government	• Implicit backing of the federal government

RECOMMENDATIONS

This chapter has focused on using commonsense techniques for describing and assessing callable agency, and summarized their advantages and disadvantages relative to bullet Treasuries. If you are a fund manager or fund supervisor, you're probably wondering what this means for your portfolio. Here are our recommendations, giving due consideration to the political issues faced by Main Street fund managers.

Generally, a manager should consider callable agencies when higher current income is a primary goal. Not only do agencies (as a class) pay more than Treasuries, but callable agencies provide a higher yield than bullet agencies. This higher income is helpful on the political front, especially when people are clamoring for better income performance.

The major negative of callable agencies, of course, is that they can be called away, forcing the manager to reinvest at a lower rate, resulting in reduced income for the budget. We recommend these tactics for dealing with the negatives of callable agencies:

- Don't overconcentrate—diversify. If callables are a reasonable proportion of the entire portfolio, the pain of reinvesting at a lower rate will not be felt.
- All things being equal, trade off more reinvestment risk for less interest-rate risk. Reinvestment risk threatens income but interest-rate risk threatens principal.
- Increase callable allocations when the interest-rate forecast calls for steady or moderately rising rates.
- Callable bonds, if used for cash management, should be positioned by maturity, not by call date. The portfolio manager should be indifferent if a bond is called before maturity. Practitioners should refrain from thinking a bond that has been called in the past will be called in the future.
- If you are thinking in terms of a ladder portfolio, ladder both lockouts and maturity. We suggest once liquidity has been maturity matched, a portfolio utilizing laddering strategies should focus on duration ladders, not just maturities.
- Avoid continuously callable agencies whenever you have a choice. These pay a little more than discrete and one-time versions, but they expose the fund to a call every day after the lockout period has expired.

And, as a final comment, always remember on Main Street price and value are not always synonymous. The features of a security affect political and economic risk, which are components of value for the Main Street investor.

POINTS TO REMEMBER

- Traditional callable securities are issued with continuous, discrete, or one-time structures.
- Lockout refers to the period of call protection following issuance of the security.
- Information on most newly issued agency securities can be found on Bloomberg's New Issue Monitor (NIM), page 2.
- Value is assessed in terms of the amount, timing, and certainty of cash flows.
- Interest-rate risk represents the highest political risk to Main Street investors.
- In making trade-offs, public fund investors should always favor principal certainty over income certainty.
- A continuous call structure results in the *least* certain cash flow since it affords so many call opportunities to the issuer. In most cases, the extra yield offered in return for this uncertainty is inadequate. The author favors discrete and one-time structures.

CHAPTER 10

Public Fund Analytics

Buying bonds is the easy part. Explaining why—now that's the hard part.

— BEN FINKELSTEIN

KEY POINTS COVERED IN THIS CHAPTER

- Applying relative value analysis to various/unique securities
- Determining the right level of liquidity
- Forecasting the market rate of return
- Forecasting portfolio income, considering pending maturities and possible calls
- Optimizing the portfolio through security purchases and rebalancing activities

This chapter presents a number of analytical techniques for portfolio management. Their primary function is to convert data into information that fund managers can use to make decisions and produce reports. Some rely on software that extracts raw data from various market sources and arrays it in ways to give managers the insights they need to do their jobs. Accounting systems and data services like Bloomberg, for example, accumulate raw data and convert it into information that can be used to assess portfolio positions against investment policy constraints and investment plan goals. That same information is then used to forecast the performance of individual securities and the portfolio as a whole.

In the pages that follow we use sample portfolio reports to demonstrate how a portfolio manager can use state-of-the-art analytics to create a user-friendly and relevant public fund framework for making investment decisions. Because there is no universal standard for suitability, readers should factor their own notions of risk and reward into this framework. Our goal throughout is to illustrate how information can be organized to reflect investment priorities more realistically.

UNDERSTANDING RELATIVE VALUE

Relative value is a tool utilized by money managers to evaluate a security's value relative to alternative securities. Wall Street managers use this tool to determine which securities are most likely to outperform the market indexes that galvanize their attention and against which their performance is measured. But, as we will see, the concept of relative value should take the Main Street practitioner along a very different path.

What is *relative value?* We define it as the spread between one security's yield and the yield on another security. For example, consider a U.S. Agency bullet with a 3-year maturity yielding 4.0 percent. Assuming a U.S. Treasury with the same maturity is yielding 3.8 percent, the relative spread is 20 basis points (4.0 minus 3.8). That spread represents the value the market is placing on differences in credit and marketability risk between these two securities. Remember that agencies, unlike Treasuries, are not backed by the full faith and credit of the U.S. federal government. Nor is agency debt as liquid—there are not as many buyers of agency debt as of Treasury debt. The spread, then, is how the market compensates the agency investor for this greater credit and liquidity risk. The question the investor must answer is straightforward: Am I getting what I'm paying for in terms of more credit risk and less liquidity? In our example, the investor might ask, Does 20 basis points in this circumstance represent fair compensation? Why not 15 basis points, or 30, or even 40?

One approach to answering these questions is to examine the historical relationship between the two securities in question—in this case, the 3-year agency bullet and the 3-year Treasury. Wall Street analysts look at the spread over some span of time: days, weeks, months, or even years. In some cases moving averages or highs and lows are the tea leaves used to analyze the spread. Some examine the spread between agencies and any number of investment-grade corporate bonds. In our example of the 20 basis points spread, looking back 90 days might reveal a 25 basis point spread. Since the current spread is lower, relatively speaking (20 versus 25 basis points), the price relatively speaking is higher, or "richer." If the Wall Street portfolio manager believes the spread will return to 25 basis points, he would most likely respond by selling agencies and buying Treasuries. Or he might simply stay in cash in anticipation of a wider spread. If rates remained unchanged but spreads moved from the current 20 to 25 basis points, this sagacious manager would outperform the index against which his performance is gauged.

Should you, as a public fund manager, care about winning this game? Rarely. Managers of public funds seldom assume the trader's role. Investment policy does not encourage speculation, and is seldom driven by total return. Its objectives are safety, liquidity, and income—in that order. Total return is not the goal.

DETERMINING THE APPROPRIATE
LEVEL OF LIQUIDITY

Back in chapter 4 we recommended the creation of a separate liquidity portfolio within the larger portfolio. Further, we suggested this liquidity portfolio be structured in two parts: primary and secondary (or backup). We need to mention, however, how the amount placed in these liquidity buckets should be determined. We do that here.

How much liquidity does a fund need to be safe? Well, there should be enough to meet forecasted, with an eye on unanticipated, needs—but not too much, since liquid funds are a less productive source of income. Here, analytics comes to our aid, giving us a structured approach to making a smart decision.

We use an Excel-based tool called the Liquidity Estimator to determine the most suitable level of portfolio liquidity. This dynamic tool can help a manager establish, monitor, and justify the public fund's current liquidity level. To use the Liquidity Estimator first gather the following data:

- The fund's cash balance at the end of each of the previous 36 months
- The previous 36 months' expenditures (calculated monthly), excluding nonrecurring operational disbursements

- Revenues received during each of the previous 36 months (again, monthly), excluding nonrecurring revenue collections, large asset sales, etc.

Once you have captured the data, you're ready for the first liquidity check. From your data select the following:

- The largest monthly deficit (revenues less disbursements) during the past 12 months, and
- The largest monthly deficit during the past 36 months

Assuming no important changes in liquidity demands, these deficits indicate normal and expected liquidity parameters for which the fund must prepare.

But what if events conspired to hit the fund with adversity on three fronts at once? What if the fund experienced its lowest cash balance, its lowest revenues, and its highest expenditures in the *same* month—the worst-case scenario? To measure that worst-case scenario, use the following data:

- The lowest fund bank balance over the previous 12 months
- The largest disbursement over the previous 12 months
- The lowest revenues collected in the previous 12 months

Once you have these data, make the following calculation:

	Lowest bank balance during the 12-month period
Plus	+ Lowest revenue collected in any single month (of the past 12)
Less	− Highest expenditure total in any single month (of the past 12)

Equals = Worst-case liquidity scenario for the past 12-month period

Now do the same calculation using figures from the past 36 months.

These worst-case figures are every fund manager's "perfect storm" nightmare, bringing together the lowest standing bank balance with the lowest revenue month and the highest expenditure month. What is the likelihood these three "storms" will converge on your fund during a single budget year? Not very likely. Nevertheless, a perfect storm scenario should be the starting point for figuring how much should be available in the primary liquidity subportfolio, and how much in the secondary subportfolio. By bracketing the normal deficit with the perfect storm deficit, you can better gauge the amount of liquidity the fund should maintain. Investment committee members should be engaged in this effort.

Let's try this perfect storm calculation for a 36-month period, using the data in Exhibit 10-1, which contains the cash balances, receipts, expenditures, and net cash flow for a hypothetical fund from November 2001 through October 2004. Exhibit 10-2 brings these figures together.

EXHIBIT 10-1
HYPOTHETICAL CASH DATA

Month	Bank Balance	Receipt	Expenditure	Net Flow
November-01	$11,721,381	$26,093,803	$25,403,907	$689,896
December-01	$15,121,381	$36,240,250	$33,883,021	$2,357,229
January-02	$19,382,566	$24,452,421	$37,035,961	$(12,583,540)
February-02	$19,882,566	$27,164,725	$26,877,524	$287,201
March-02	$28,982,566	$41,943,981	$31,571,695	$10,372,286
April-02	$37,851,528	$49,978,239	$34,486,913	$15,491,326
May-02	$27,951,528	$27,413,299	$36,129,651	$(8,716,352)
June-02	$20,951,528	$27,368,458	$34,903,560	$(7,535,102)
July-02	$27,553,576	$36,149,034	$39,658,626	$(3,509,592)
August-02	$25,653,576	$33,075,129	$39,076,986	$(6,001,857)
September-02	$31,253,576	$33,732,627	$29,850,204	$3,882,423
October-02	$27,453,576	$19,430,352	$27,576,499	$(8,146,147)
November-02	$35,218,670	$22,694,149	$24,199,131	$(1,504,982)
December-02	$29,018,670	$36,927,688	$37,692,658	$(764,970)
January-03	$31,671,314	$34,641,469	$34,060,513	$580,956
February-03	$37,871,314	$38,350,115	$31,405,752	$6,944,363
March-03	$26,371,314	$23,181,838	$34,077,986	$(10,896,148)
April-03	$38,025,510	$40,852,304	$25,505,473	$15,346,831
May-03	$35,525,510	$42,356,312	$29,187,251	$13,169,061
June-03	$36,525,510	$21,284,240	$36,397,666	$(15,113,426)
July-03	$30,175,181	$39,643,104	$43,534,939	$(3,891,835)
August-03	$34,175,181	$32,160,936	$32,444,754	$(283,818)
September-03	$39,975,181	$32,591,583	$31,359,939	$1,231,644
October-03	$39,611,849	$31,257,951	$38,045,563	$(6,787,612)
November-03	$34,411,849	$34,851,093	$25,825,386	$9,025,707
December-03	$39,911,849	$41,650,510	$36,090,139	$5,560,371
January-04	$30,828,246	$35,549,972	$24,232,113	$11,317,859
February-04	$35,528,246	$28,727,660	$34,228,731	$(5,501,071)
March-04	$34,525,246	$38,419,096	$43,140,816	$(4,721,720)
April-04	$37,648,685	$47,924,990	$28,386,140	$19,538,850
May-04	$34,648,685	$35,264,593	$33,625,887	$1,638,706
June-04	$19,248,685	$29,759,647	$35,941,412	$(6,181,765)
July-04	$19,358,215	$33,925,981	$40,956,961	$(7,030,980)
August-04	$25,458,215	$33,716,799	$31,622,588	$2,094,211
September-04	$27,058,215	$35,125,711	$32,890,435	$2,235,276
October-04	$17,148,965	$18,953,707	$29,501,134	$(10,547,427)

EXHIBIT 10-2
PERFECT STORM CALCULATION (36-MONTH PERIOD)

	Lowest bank balance during the 36-month period	$11,721,381
Plus	+ Lowest revenue collected in any single month (of the past 36)	18,953,707
Less	– Highest expenditure total in any single month (of the past 36)	43,534,939
Equals	= Worst-case liquidity scenario	$(12,859,851)

Should the fund keep $12.8 million in the primary liquidity portfolio on the off chance that a perfect storm will hit? Maybe. Maybe not. Just knowing what the magnitude of the worst case, however, can help people get to a reasonable decision.

An alternative to the perfect storm method is to look back over recent years to identify monthly variances from annual budget forecasts. If the highest variance from forecast is, say, 40 percent, that could be taken as the worst-case scenario and a guide to discussion of current fund liquidity. Simply put, this type of quantitative evaluation provides a basis for discussion and support for liquidity levels.

FORECASTING THE MARKET RATE OF RETURN

From liquidity, we turn to income. Every public fund is charged with obtaining a market rate of return on behalf of its stakeholders. The typical policy language says something to this effect: "The investment portfolio seeks a market rate of return throughout changing budgetary and economic cycles, within constraints of investment risk and liquidity needs." Fine, but what standard should a fund set for its market rate of return, and how can it know if its portfolio will deliver? Again, analytics helps us answer these questions.

Consider the case of the City of Suntown, which has chosen the 12-month moving average of the 2-year monthly CMT (constant maturity treasury) yield[1] as its market rate of return benchmark and duration benchmark. There are three reasons for this choice:

1. By looking back over ten years and calculating the annualized return across the Treasury curve, supervisors of the Suntown fund recognized the 2-year USTN provided an excellent risk/return trade-off, providing 70 percent of the 30-year yield with 23 percent of the risk, as measured by standard deviation (see this discussion under opportunity cost in chapter 6). The portfolio's price risk or duration is 1.80, approximating the price risk of the 2-year USTN.

2. A 12-month moving average reflects the typical budget cycle.

3. A moving average more realistically reflects the passive activity of buying and selling securities within the portfolio. Unlike monthly total return indexes, where price change dominates performance reporting, a moving average reinforces the focus on budget stability and not market volatility.

But why use a 12-month moving average when choosing a 2-year maturity? Because it provides the investment team with an early warning system for interest rate changes. Also, the 12-month moving average creates the most logical and relevant way for keeping a portfolio producing a market rate of return through economic cycles.

Once the market rate benchmark and duration have been selected, we are able to forecast the rate over our planning period. To do that we must make some assumptions about the future moves in the federal funds rate. Exhibit 10-3 is an example of the spreadsheet treatment we use to forecast the market rate of return for a particular portfolio.

In the exhibit, in December of 2004 we assumed the Federal Reserve will raise rates by 25 basis points six times between January 31 and September 30, 2005. The point of this forecast is to prod the practitioner to consider what adjustments in current strategy may be necessary to maintain a budget reflective of these market conditions.

Notice that by the end of December 31, 2005 (assuming this forecast is reasonably accurate) the 12-month moving average of the market rate of return will have moved from 2.52 percent to 3.84 percent. At 3.84 percent, portfolio earnings will be underperforming the market rate of return by 63 basis points (3.84 minus 3.21). This forecast gives the portfolio manager the required time to consider options and develop a strategy to prudently increase the portfolio's purchase yield. This is in contrast to the Wall Street approach. Wall Street concentrates on total return and short-term trading

EXHIBIT 10-3
MARKET RATE OF RETURN FORECAST

Inputs		USER INPUTS			
3.21	Current Purchase Yield		Minimum Spread:		25
50	Target Spread to 2Yr CMT 12Mo Avg		Median Spread:		50
$1,761	Portfolio Size ($MM)		Maximum Spread:		75
$381	Total Cash ($MM)		3Mo to 2Yr Tsy Spread(bp):		
$150	Cash Floor ($MM)				

12-Month Horizon	Fed Rate Hikes	Fed Funds	2-Year CMT Spread to Fed Funds*	2-Year CMT Forecast	12-Month Moving Average of 2-Year CMT	Purchase Yield Do-Nothing	Purchase Yield Spread to 12-Month Moving Average of 2-Year CMT	Minimum Spread Purchase Yield	Median Spread Purchase Yield	Maximum Spread Purchase Yield
01/31/2005		2.25	0.80	3.05	2.52	3.21	0.69	2.77	3.02	3.27
02/28/2005	25	2.50	0.78	3.28	2.65	3.21	0.67	2.90	3.15	3.40
03/31/2005	25	2.75	0.75	3.50	2.81	3.21	0.66	3.06	3.31	3.56
04/30/2005		2.75	0.72	3.47	2.91	3.21	0.64	3.16	3.41	3.66
05/31/2005	25	3.00	0.69	3.69	3.01	3.21	0.62	3.26	3.51	3.76
06/30/2005	25	3.25	0.67	3.92	3.11	3.21	0.60	3.36	3.61	3.86
07/31/2005		3.25	0.64	3.89	3.21	3.21	0.59	3.46	3.71	3.96
08/31/2005	25	3.50	0.61	4.11	3.35	3.21	0.57	3.60	3.85	4.10
09/30/2005	25	3.75	0.58	4.33	3.49	3.21	0.55	3.74	3.99	4.24
10/31/2005		3.75	0.56	4.31	3.64	3.21	0.53	3.89	4.14	4.39
11/30/2005	0	3.75	0.53	4.28	3.74	3.21	0.52	3.99	4.24	4.49
12/31/2005	0	3.75	0.50	4.25	3.84	3.21	0.50	4.09	4.34	4.59

*Assumptions: 2-Year CMT spread to Fed Funds converges to 50bps. 10-Year historical average spread is 40bps.

strategies to outperform an index; Main Street uses a market rate of return to provide stability and optimize the income available to future budgets.

FUTURE INCOME FORECASTING

The third analytical tool in our tool kit focuses on the anticipated impact of maturing and called bonds on future portfolio earnings. Remember, maturing and called bonds put cash into our hands, but this must be reinvested at whatever rates are available at the time. Will the resulting income be sufficient to meet the demands of the budget?

To begin, imagine a portfolio containing one bond with a par amount of $1 million. That security was issued as a 1.5-year bond with a purchase yield of 5 percent. The fund manager is not an active trader; nor does he follow a strict buy-and-hold strategy. Instead, he follows a strategy of passive management, rebalancing when doing so is appropriate and consistent with the investment plan.

During the first year, market rates remain unchanged and the portfolio contributes 5 percent (the purchase yield) to the budget. In the eleventh month, rates on 1.5-year bonds drop to 3 percent. There are now six months left to maturity. Now, the next year's budget comes around and the purchase yield on the portfolio is currently 5 percent. But unless rates rise in six months the fund will have to reinvest at a lower rate. Alternatively, if the bond is callable, it now may be redeemed by the issuer prior to maturity. How can the manager know how much income will be available through the new budget year? (Naturally, this problem is more complex when a portfolio contains many securities, each with a different maturity, purchase yield, and call feature.) A buy-and-hold portfolio manager would be oblivious to this problem. He would submit 5 percent as the spendable income for the next year's budget. Of course, in six months his bond will mature or be called, and he will have to reinvest at 3 percent. The result: a blended rate of 4 percent for the budget year. This is a simple example, but it gets to the heart of the problem that income forecast analysis is designed to address.

So where does this leave us? Using our Liquidity Estimator, we established appropriate liquidity levels the portfolio must set aside. The balance of the portfolio will then be invested for income consistent with the investment plan. As time marches forward, the portfolio purchase yield will change due to called bonds, maturing bonds, and changing reinvestment rates. Our market rate of return forecasting tool (Exhibit 10-3) has already quantified what the future may look like compared to where we are today, and what must be done to maintain or improve our market rate of return target. The income forecast tool provides insights into the impact of these changes on the portfolio purchase yield and, more important, helps the fund manager determine which bonds should be purchased given one of three scenarios: falling rates, unchanged rates, or rising rates.

Exhibit 10-4 shows what a sample public fund portfolio would be expected to produce over a 12-month period. To keep it simple, we focus our analysis on the 12-month scenario.

In this example the market value of the Dry Gulch County Water District Fund is about $90 million. Its purchase yield is 2.93 percent. As a California public fund, it can invest in the Local Agency Investment Fund (LAIF), an authorized government investment pool which is currently yielding 1.45 percent. The fund's manager has made three interest-rate forecasts: a drop of 25 basis points (bps); no change; and a rate rise of 100 bps. Looking at the 12-month horizon in the exhibit, we notice that if rates remained unchanged, $40 million of the $90 million portfolio will either mature or be called (the analytical model contains the maturity schedules and assumes bond calls in response to interest rate changes). With the $17 million it already has in LAIF, the portfolio would be expected to have more than 65 percent in cash or LAIF by the end of the period. More important, the $40 million block that will mature or be called has a purchase yield of 3.41 percent. Cash from maturities and calls will end up in LAIF at a meager 1.45 percent, giving the overall portfolio a purchase yield of 2.04 percent—substantially less than the current 2.93 percent. These developments will have a major impact on the fund's income; we would expect that income to drop 35 percent, from $2.65 million to $1.85 million, based on the analysis.

The benefit of this analytical tool is that it provides fund managers with a practical way to anticipate how portfolio earnings will change with changing market conditions.

EXHIBIT 10-4
FUTURE INCOME FORECASTING

INCOME FORECAST AUG 25 04
HORIZON REQUIRED YIELD ANALYSIS
ANALYSIS DATE 8/25/04

Total Mkt Value:	90,508	
Total Par Value:	89,759	
Current Purchase Yield:	2.93%	
Target Purchase Yield:	2.93%	
LAIF Current Earns:	1.45%	

	Current	12Mo Forecast		
		−25bp	Unchng	+100bp
LAIF	17,423	17,423	17,423	17,423
MATURED	0	43,750	40,750	21,250
TOTAL	17,423	61,173	58,173	38,673
% of Port	19%	68%	65%	43%
% Mat/Cld		49%	45%	24%
Abs Pur Yld Lost	1.45%	3.36%	3.41%	3.49%
Wtgd Pur Yld Lost	0.28%	1.64%	1.55%	0.83%
Port Pur Yld*	2.93%	1.83%	2.04%	2.88%
Required Yld		3.46%	3.41%	2.67%

*Assumes that the Pur Yld Lost (that portion of the portfolio that is called or matured) is reinvested into LAIF which is adjusted for the rate change. Required Yld applies to amount called/matured.

A PLAN STATUS REPORT

Each of the analytical tools we've described so far has focused on a specific dimension of portfolio performance. We now turn to something that provides a broader picture.

The dashboard in your car has several status and performance indicators: the speedometer, odometer, fuel gauge, tachometer, and so forth. These give you continuous feedback about the performance of your vehicle. You can build something similar for your portfolio—a panel of gauges that quantify the situation relative to the investment plan and policy constraints. We call this the Investment Plan Status Report. Exhibit 10-5 is an example for the City of Prudence fund. This report, done up in a computer spreadsheet, puts all key indicators in one place, making review, evaluation, and monitoring easy. It reports three parameters of interest to the fund

EXHIBIT 10-5

INVESTMENT PLAN STATUS REPORT

Prepared for: **City of Prudence**   Prepared by: **Good Stewardship**

LIQUIDITY	PORTFOLIO	PLAN	VARIANCE
CASH	14.72	9.96	4.76
0 - 1 YRS	10.59	5.98	4.61
TOTAL	25.31	15.94	9.37

Portfolio Par Value$(000):	$100,929
Portfolio Market Value$(000):	$101,437
Portfolio Book Value$(000):	$101,394
Gain/Loss $(000):	$(744)

FUNDAMENTALS	PORTFOLIO	PLAN	VARIANCE
AVG COUPON	3.79	3.83	(0.04)
AVG MATURITY	2.02	2.36	(0.34)
AVG QUALITY	Aa1	Aa1	
PUR YIELD/MktRtn	3.52	2.92	0.60
EFF DURATION	1.34	1.70	(0.36)
CONVEXITY	(0.32)	(0.27)	(0.05)

*Pur Yield is Wgtd Avg Yld using original cost & purchase date
*MktRtn is the Market Rate of Return(12 Month Avg of 2Yr CMT)

DURATION	PORTFOLIO	PLAN	VARIANCE
CASH	14.72	10.06	4.66
0 - 1 YRS	14.09	12.44	1.65
1 - 2 YRS	49.70	44.48	5.22
2 - 3 YRS	21.50	19.56	1.94
3 - 4 YRS	0.00	11.16	(11.16)
4 - 5 YRS	0.00	2.26	(2.26)
5 - 6 YRS	0.00	0.00	0.00
6 - 7 YRS	0.00	0.00	0.00
7 - 8 YRS	0.00	0.00	0.00
8 - 9 YRS	0.00	0.00	0.00
9 - 10 YRS	0.00	0.00	0.00
10 + YRS	0.00	0.00	0.00

SECTOR	PORTFOLIO	PLAN	VARIANCE
Cash/MM	14.72	9.96	4.76
US Treasury	0.00	4.99	(4.99)
US Agency	64.93	55.08	9.85
US Agency Bullets	*21.17*	*5.00*	*16.17*
US Agency Callables	*39.82*	*50.08*	*(10.26)*
US Agency Structure	*3.94*	*0.00*	*3.94*
US Pass-Thru	0.00	0.00	0.00
US ABS	0.00	0.00	0.00
US Corporates	20.35	29.97	(9.62)
US Corp Industrial	*0.00*	*9.10*	*(9.10)*
US Corp Finance	*18.42*	*19.74*	*(1.32)*
Other Corp	*1.93*	*1.13*	*0.80*
OTHER	0.00	0.00	0.00

MATURITY	PORTFOLIO	PLAN	VARIANCE
CASH	14.72	9.96	4.76
0 - 1 YRS	10.59	5.98	4.61
1 - 2 YRS	26.46	25.36	1.10
2 - 3 YRS	18.39	25.23	(6.84)
3 - 4 YRS	23.36	17.67	5.69
4 - 5 YRS	6.48	15.79	(9.31)
5 - 7 YRS	0.00	0.00	0.00
7 - 10 YRS	0.00	0.00	0.00
10 - 15 YRS	0.00	0.00	0.00
15 - 20 YRS	0.00	0.00	0.00
20 - 25 YRS	0.00	0.00	0.00
25+ YRS	0.00	0.00	0.00

Pricing/Analysis Date: **04/25/05**

PORTFOLIO SENSITIVITY ANALYSIS			
Instantaneous	–25bp	Unchanged	+100bp
Effective Duration	1.26	1.34	1.63
Convexity	(0.33)	(0.32)	(0.20)
3 Month Horizon	–25bp	Unchanged	+100bp
Effective Duration	1.12	1.19	1.50
Convexity	(0.27)	(0.28)	(0.12)
Forecasted Pyld	3.29	3.38	3.66
$ Called/Matured	11,500	9,500	0
12 Month Horizon	–25bp	Unchanged	+100bp
Effective Duration	0.83	0.91	1.15
Convexity	(0.11)	(0.12)	(0.07)
Forecasted Pyld	2.80	3.03	3.48
$ Called/Matured	32,000	24,000	10,500

managers and fund supervisors: status relative to plan, the risk level, and sensitivity in interest rate fluctuations, as measured by effective duration. These indicate how well the plan is working relative to the fund's key obligations, and produce an easy monitor to insure investment practice follows policy.

Liquidity

The first step to take with this decision dashboard is to look at the liquidity level of the existing portfolio. This is found in the left-hand side of the report's top section. Portfolio liquidity is indicated as a percentage of the portfolio's market value and indicates the liquidity variance from the investment plan. Quantities bracketed by parentheses are negative values. Negative values act as warning lights, telling the fund manager to begin rebuilding liquidity. In the example one can see the portfolio's primary liquidity and secondary liquidity exceed the investment plan's targeted level of 9.96 percent and 5.98 percent respectively.

Once liquidity is insured, the next step is to compare the credit and interest-rate risk of the portfolio compared to the stated parameters of the investment plan. Returning to the top section of the report, on the right side, we find that all is in order. The average credit quality of the portfolio is equal to the investment plan of Aa1. Interest-rate risk is captured in line item labeled "Eff Duration" (effective duration), which shows the portfolio's effective duration (1.34) is below—that is, less risky than—the effective duration specified in the investment plan (1.70). This variance should motivate the fund manager to take action to increase the overall interest-rate risk of the portfolio.

Our decision dashboard serves two useful purposes. First, it helps the fund manager and fund supervisors keep an eye on the portfolio's suitability. Every variance alerts them to potential problems. Second, it provides insights into the type of investments that would serve the requirements of the investment plan. In a sense, it acts as a source of objective feedback.

Risk and Structure

The middle section of Exhibit 10-5 provides an indication of the riskiness of the portfolio and how it is structured. The left-hand side of this middle section contains the risk measurement (effective duration), and the right-hand side summarizes how the portfolio is structured in terms of types—callables, bullets, Treasuries, and so forth. Better still, these risks and structure values are compared to the investment plan, and variances from the plan are clearly indicated. This type of summary information is invaluable to anyone who needs fast feedback about the status of the portfolio and how well it matches up with the investment plan. For the portfolio in the exhibit, we see evidence of adequate liquidity and effective duration within the risk tolerance of the investment plan's benchmark. Based on the data in the report, the manager should buy securities in the 2 to 3, 3 to 4, or 4 to 5 effective duration bucket. Looking at the agency and corporate sections, we see the manager could make future purchases in these categories and still be within the plan. (Note: the numbers in this section—such as 49.70—indicate the percentage of portfolio market value represented by each of the different security types).

Sensitivity Analysis

The bottom section of the decision dashboard addresses the sensitivity of the portfolio to changing interest rates. The left side of this bottom section indicates the asset quantities allocated by maturity (average life, if a mortgage). We can see some maturities are overweighted (those with positive variances) while others are underweighted (negative variances). We include this section of the report for those public funds that continue to use average life rather than duration as their indicator of interest-rate risk. Average life is not the measure we recommend, but we recognize that many funds use it.

The right hand of the bottom section, Portfolio Sensitivity Analysis, quantifies the portfolio's income sensitivity to changes in interest rates over 3- and 12-month time frames. This is a condensed version of the income forecasting discussed earlier.

The Investment Plan Status Report helps the public fund manager bring together the often conflicting demands of politics and economics. It does this by comparing the actual portfolio to the investment plan, the latter being a market-wise reflection of investment policy. Since the plan defines what is suitable, variance from plan indicates departures from what has been deemed suitable. **In this sense, the Investment Plan Status Report provides a very user-friendly way for fund personnel to combine politics with state-of-the-art analytics.**

OPTIMIZING THE PORTFOLIO

To *optimize* is to implement the best possible solution to a problem that contains conflicting issues. When we seek to optimize a portfolio, we face conflicts among safety, liquidity, and income. For example, we would like to put everything into long-term bonds to get the highest return, but doing so would jeopardize safety of principal. The constraints of investment policy also enter the picture. As with life, portfolio management forces us to make trade-offs. Practitioners find they must forgo the "perfect" in favor of the "good."

The tools in this chapter (exhibits 10-1 through 10-5) are valuable on a stand-alone basis. They can help you make better decisions with respect to liquidity levels, forecasting the market rate of return, forecasting portfolio income, and seeing at a glance how you're doing relative to your investment plan. Best of all, you can use our examples as templates for building your own spreadsheet-based versions of these tools. But wouldn't it be great if you had a tool to optimize these different dimensions of your portfolio? We have built a dynamic program for doing just that. We call it the Main Street Optimization Framework, or MSOF. It modifies Wall Street to the needs of Main Street by focusing on optimizing a market rate of return rather than total return, and making it possible for the Main Street practitioner to manage the investment portfolio with limited time, resources, and staff.

We use the MSOF routinely in our work with public funds. Unfortunately, the spreadsheet outputs of the program are very large, and the details of explaining and interpreting them are beyond the scope of this book. It is possible and useful, however, to give an overview of the optimization process enabled by this program.

A key goal of the MSOF is to identify individual securities that, when blended into the current portfolio, will produce the optimum market rate of return given the defined safety, liquidity, and income parameters. It answers these four critical questions:

1. Do we have money not earmarked for liquidity to invest?
2. If so, what are the right bonds to produce the optimal market rate of return?
3. How do we choose between investing cash and rebalancing the portfolio, where rebalancing means maintaining a market rate of return?
4. If we rebalance the portfolio, which are the right securities to sell?

Together, these questions move the practitioner away from buying individual bonds to managing a portfolio.

The answer to question 1 comes directly from the Investment Plan Status Report (see Exhibit 10-5). There, a positive variance indicates more cash than needed to cover targeted primary and secondary liquidity. That excess is available to invest right now.

The other three questions are more challenging. Our Main Street Optimization Framework uses two worksheets—an optimization worksheet and a rebalancing worksheet—to answer them.

Optimization Worksheet

The optimization worksheet converts Wall Street tools into a suite of tools designed to comprehensively identify the securities that should be purchased with available cash, and how those purchases will impact the total portfolio risk/reward profile. The worksheet has three steps:

1. Prepurchase review
2. Optimization candidates
3. Results

Prepurchase review Prepurchase review gives a snapshot of the before-and-after results of optimization. The program operates within the fund's policy constraints and a range of interest rate changes forecasted by the analyst. For example, it might indicate the current portfolio purchase yield is 3.51 percent, but would increase to 3.62 if optimization recommendations were followed.

Optimization candidates Prepurchase review draws on the set of securities using different market prices obtained from dealers. The data associated with these candidate securities includes everything you'd need to evaluate their impact on the portfolio: coupon rates, maturities, effective durations, prices, yields, and types (such as callable agency). The program will automatically calculate the impact of the analyst's assumed interest-rate changes on the price and yield of each of these securities.

Key to an optimization effectiveness is that the candidate securities must be real offerings with current market pricing. The program is extremely flexible. It allows the practitioner to filter candidates based on preselected securities or structures. For example, continuous callable securities could be excluded automatically.

Results The results section of the optimization worksheet provides the user an "after we bought" glimpse of the portfolio. The power of this prepurchase analysis is to allow the portfolio manager to test his or her strategy at a portfolio level using various complex security structures before having to pull the trigger. All of the essential inputs found on the previously mentioned planning dashboard are displayed in the optimization worksheet. It is a marvelously simple and effective way of applying science to the art of portfolio management.

Rebalancing Worksheet

The opening quote of this chapter noted that buying bonds is the easy part; explaining why is harder. The same holds true for selling. This should be clear from chapter 7, where profiting from losses was discussed. It's not an easy story to tell to a fund overseer.

Now that we know what we should buy for the portfolio, it's time to determine what we should sell—and why. The why of selling is easy for the Wall Street practitioner, who sells to increase total return. But we're after a market rate of return, which complicates matters. Fortunately, the rebalancing worksheet of the MSOF can help us find the best sell-side securities.

Rebalancing is periodically necessary to keep the portfolio aligned with the investment plan. Some public fund managers resist this idea, confusing it with trading. Others view rebalancing narrowly—and incorrectly; they adhere to the folksy (but false) advice of "sell your winners and hold your losers."

Rebalancing should follow a discipline that maintains the portfolio's purchase yield at the prevailing market rate of return. This implies that as budgetary and economic cycles change, the portfolio remains aligned with those changes. Typically a rebalance will seek to achieve this market balance by removing inferior bonds from the existing portfolio. An inferior bond is defined as a bond whose purchase yield is below the portfolio's purchase yield but whose loss, when realized, will be recovered within the stated time constraints.

Optimization works at the portfolio macro level in helping to identify and establish which securities should be chosen or bought to achieve the desired strategy. A rebalance strategy will screen sell-side candidates both individually and in aggregate using the optimization's recommended buy-side candidates. This sell-side or micro level perspective will select only sell-side candidates whose realized loss can be recovered and, when replaced with buy-side candidates, produce an income enhancement within the preferred time horizon.

An example of the rebalance worksheet search criteria would be to find existing bonds with purchase yields below the weighted average purchase yield of the current portfolio. It then confirms that the optimized buy-side candidate will, if purchased with the proceeds from the sell-side candidate, make up the loss either before the first call date or maturity date of the sell-side candidate. While the rebalance is done in aggregate using multiple sell and buy-side securities, the analysis can be broken down into individual securities to confirm the breakeven take-out yields, income advantage, and principal recovery.

In conclusion, the Main Street Optimization Framework provides the discipline (keeping current portfolio aligned with investment plan) and analytics to select the optimal buy and sell securities. In addition, MSOF corrects the error of thinking that gains are always good and losses are always bad. The public fund that embraces MSOF will no longer relegate its investment strategy or discipline to an ad hoc habit of buying single securities to fill gaps resulting from maturities. Instead, it will keep a sharp edge on the portfolio, making it the best it can be, given policy directives and constraints and budget needs.

POINTS TO REMEMBER

- Relative value is a tool used to determine one security's yield relative to the yield on another security. It helps the investor know whether he or she is getting a fair return, given credit risk and liquidity issues.
- The Liquidity Estimator is a tool for determining the needed level of fund liquidity given past ending cash balances, expenditures, and revenues.
- Public fund managers are obliged to seek a market rate of return. The 12-month moving average of the 2-year CMT is often used for this rate. The Market Rate of Return Forecast tool can be used to estimate how that rate will change over the fund's planning horizon.
- The Future Income Forecasting tool is used to anticipate the impact of maturing and called bonds on future portfolio earnings.
- The Investment Plan Status Report reports three parameters of importance to fund managers and fund supervisors: status relative to plan, the risk level, and sensitivity to interest rate fluctuations as measured by effective duration. Taken together, these indicate how well the plan is working relative to the fund's policy and portfolio.
- The Main Street Optimization Framework, or MSOF, is used to identify individual securities that, when blended into the current portfolio, will produce the optimal market rate of return given the portfolio's defined safety, liquidity, and income parameters.

GLOSSARY

Accrued interest The interest that has accumulated on a bond since the last interest payment, up to but not including the settlement date.

Agency bonds (aka agencies) These bonds include such agencies as Fannie Mae, Freddie Mac, Sallie Mae, and the Federal Home Loan Banks. They do not include those issued by the U.S. Treasury or by municipalities.

Amortized cost For a fixed-income security, it is the par value of the investment increased or decreased by any unamortized premium or discount. Amortized cost accounting ignores the mark-to-market change in value due that results when interest rates change. An important implication for public funds trying to avoid GASB 31 mark-to-market requirements is to keep purchases of fixed-income securities 12 months or less. Securities that qualify under GASB 31 that are held 12 months or less can be reported at their amortized cost.

Average life An indicator of when the investor's principal will be repaid. Many fund managers use average life to measure their price volatility of securities or portfolios.

Basis point In reference to bond yields, 1/100 percent (i.e., 0.01 percent). Thus, 50 basis points equal 0.5 percent.

Bear market For fixed-income securities, a period when yields are rising and bond prices are falling.

Bermuda structure See Discrete structure.

Bullet A noncallable bond. Securities whose cash flows are known with certainty (no call dates).

Bull market For fixed-income securities, a period when yields are dropping and bond prices are increasing.

Buy-and-hold investor This is an investor who is characterized by ignoring market changes and budget cycles. No strategy is employed once the security is purchased. This investor is the extreme opposite of the trader: The trader intends to sell the security before maturity; the buy and hold does nothing until the bond matures.

Callable security A security that the issuer has the right to redeem prior to maturity.

Canary A bond that is discretely callable for some initial time period, and then converts to a bullet. A canary callable can have fixed coupons or coupons that step (canary callables with coupons that step are the most common). For example, a 5-year non-call 2 year (5nc2 in market parlance) canary callable indicates a bond that is discretely callable (usually every 6 months) for the first two years and then converts, if not called, to a 3-year bullet.

Continuous structure With respect to a callable security, a structure that allows the issuer to exercise its call option any time prior to the expiration. Also called an American structure.

Credit risk The risk that a bond issuer will be unable to make timely interest payments and/or to repay the face value of its bonds at maturity. Also called default risk.

Default risk See Credit risk.

Discount bond A bond selling for less than its face value.

Discrete structure With respect to a Callable security, a structure that allows the issuer to redeem the security quarterly or on semi-annual coupon dates up to maturity.

Duration is the sensitivity of a bond's price expressed as the percentage change in price for a 100 basis point change in yield. It represents the weighted average present value of the bond's future cash flows where the present values serve as the present value weights.

Economic principal is the income earned (eggs) from investing the public fund's political principal (goose). Economic principal is the portfolio's budgeted income. An important point in differentiating economic from political principal is the former is a loss in opportunity cost (didn't make as much as we could have, an example being reinvestment risk) whereas the latter is an actual decline in the core of earning assets (portfolio had $10 million of political or original principal; now it only has $9.5 million to earn income from).

Effective duration A measure of duration that accounts for changes in expected cash flows for a security. Effective duration is one measure used in dealing with callable and mortgaged-backed securities.

European structure See One-time structure.

Federal Home Loan Mortgage Corporation (FHLMC: aka Freddie Mac) A publicly chartered agency that issues notes and bonds and lends the proceeds to mortgage lenders.

Fiduciary benchmark Unlike Wall Street, where focus is primarily on total return, a fiduciary benchmark captures all of the investment policy objectives. Through the investment plan, a public fund creates the only relevant benchmark: their investment policy. Suitability, not total return, is then used to measure performance.

Gain As defined by Wall Street and accountants, the difference between original cost or book value of a security and its market value excluding accrued interest.

Government investment pool (GIP) A state or county investment pool that public funds can use to invest assets. GIPs provide immediate liquidity and price stability.

Interest-rate risk The market price volatility that fixed-income securities experience as a consequence of changing market interest rates.

Investment plan A portfolio interpretation of the investment policy. It converts a static investment policy from a rule book to a playbook, providing a day-to-day link between investment practice and investment policy. The investment plan reflects the entity's definition of a suitable portfolio.

Investment policy A written statement of portfolio goals and the rules that must be observed in achieving those goals. In public funds, policy generally stipulates the types and percentages of securities that the portfolio may hold, and identifies the source of oversight authority and reporting requirements of the portfolio manager. The investment policy is focused on what is legal.

Laddering A fixed-income strategy wherein the manager invests all funds not required for liquidity in securities with progressively longer maturities.

Liquidation loss Unlike a recognized but unrealized loss (temporary), this is a permanent loss of a portfolio's political (original) principal. It is a loss taken only when no other option exists for the portfolio manager to pay an obligation.

Liquidity For Wall Street, it is the bid/offer spread. A measure of the ease with which an asset can be bought or sold.

Liquidity risk For Main Street, it is the ability to sell a security without realizing a principal loss.

Lockout period A period of time during which a callable security cannot be redeemed by its issuer.

Market rate of return The benchmark return used to compare the portfolio's purchase yield. Unlike total return used by Wall Street, a market rate of return uses a twelve-month moving average yield derived from one of the CMT (constant maturity treasury) maturities. A twelve-month average was chosen by the author because budgetary cycles are usually twelve months; however, other monthly averages based on some objective criteria would be appropriate.

Market yield The yield bid for a security when selling, or the yield asked for when buying.

One-time structure With respect to a Callable security, a call structure that gives the issuer the right (but not the obligation) to call the bond on one specified date. Also called European or 1-X callable bonds.

Opportunity cost The value of an alternative not taken.

Optimization A process where state-of-the-art fixed-income analytics is utilized to produce the optimum buy-side and sell-side candidates. Optimum means producing the highest market rate of return for the least amount of political and economic risk. This is typically done using two scenarios; one instantaneous and the other twelve months forward.

Paper profits and losses See Recognized profits and losses

Par bond A bond selling at its face (or par) value.

Passive investor This is an investor who periodically rebalances the portfolio to achieve a market rate of return through budget and economic cycles. The passive investor is a balance between traders and buy-and-hold investors. Unlike the trader who looks to price changes to enhance portfolio returns, the passive investor looks to capital market risk premiums such as liquidity, reinvestment, and credit risk to enhance portfolio income.

Political principal The core earning assets of the public fund. It is the asset base that the investment policy refers to when stating preservation of principal is a primary goal of public fund investment stewards. This asset base (goose) is what generates the income (eggs) for budget purposes.

Politically correct portfolio A portfolio constructed to specifically achieve the optimum balance between preservation of principal, liquidity, and income. The optimum balance is described by the public funds investment plan.

Premium bond A bond that sells for more than its face value.

Realized loss is a temporary loss of the portfolio's economic or political principal. It is recovered through a rebalance strategy when there is a simultaneous sell and repurchase of multiple securities. Realized losses are part of the passive investor's strategy of maintaining a market rate of return throughout budget and economic cycles.

Rebalance strategy A technique whereby inferior securities are chosen to sell. Rebalancing is used by passive investors of public funds to maintain the portfolio purchase yield at market rate of returns throughout budget and economic cycles.

Recognized profits and losses An accounting convention that takes note of the market-to-market value of a security. It is synonymous with the terms unrealized and paper losses or gains.

Reinvestment risk The risk that coupon payments and/or premature redemptions will have to be reinvested at lower rates of return.

Return pickup The expected economic gain, expressed in basis points, over a Take-out yield.

Risk In the world of finance, uncertainty surrounding the amount and timing of expected future cash flows.

Settlement date With respect to the sale of a security, the date on which the money and the security change hands.

Standard deviation A widely used measure of risk. It refers to the tendency of returns to cluster around an average, and represents the degree to which returns are dispersed around that average.

Step-up coupon A coupon that increases incrementally over the life of the security.

Structure For a callable agency bond, the formula used to determine the security's coupon. Fixed and step-up are two examples of structure.

Suitability The performance measure used to evaluate a public fund's investment stewardship. Suitability has five tests that must be passed to be considered; the steward must 1) demonstrate adequate liquidity to meet obligations without having to liquidate a security; 2) possess the appropriate level of interest-rate risk/duration; 3) maintain a diversified portfolio; 4) demonstrate that holdings are legal; and 5) achieve a market rate of return.

Take-out yield The market value yield on remaining cash flows. It is the minimum yield required to replace or break even on the sale of a security.

Traders Portfolio managers who intend to sell securities before maturity and profit from price moves as the primary means of enhancing portfolio return. Traders are seekers of total return.

Unrealized profits and losses See Recognized profits and losses.

CHAPTER 1

1. Peter L. Bernstein, *Capital Ideas: The Improbable Origins of Modern Wall Street* (New York: Free Press, 1992), 11–12.

CHAPTER 2

1. James P. Owen, *The Prudent Investor: The Definitive Guide to Professional Investment Management* (Chicago: Probus Publishing, 1990), 17.

2. Charles D. Ellis, *Investment Policy: How to Win the Loser's Game*, 2nd ed. (Homewood, IL: Dow Jones-Irwin, 1993), 58.

3. There are sometimes two levels of legality (such as state and city or other entity). Sometimes an entity's investment policy can be narrower than code in the investments it allows. For instance, a state law may allow corporate bonds, but a city may not have the expertise, time, or stomach to safely invest in them, so its policy excludes them. State law may allow long-term bond funds, but the city policy may only allow money funds in order to limit volatility. State law may have no limits on term, but a city policy may limit terms to three to five years.

CHAPTER 3

1. Overall variance from the mean is measured through a calculated value: standard deviation. In the example, A has larger standard deviation than does B.

CHAPTER 5

1. Ken Ward, "Missing Out on Millions—City's Money Squandering Investment Strategies," *Las Vegas Review-Journal*, 2 January 2002.

2. Statement 31 of the Governmental Accounting Standards Board, "Accounting and Financial Reporting for Certain Investments and for External Investment Pools," Governmental Accounting Standards Board of the Financial Accounting Foundation, No. 144-A, March 1997, see Summary.

3. Robert Brooks and J. Brian Gray, "History of the Forecasters," *Journal of Portfolio Management* (Fall 2004), 113–17.

CHAPTER 8

1. Marcia Stigum and Frank Fabozzi, *The Dow Jones–Irwin Guide to Bond and Money Market Investments* (Homewood, IL: Dow Jones-Irwin, 1987), 99.

2. As described by Mark Kritzman in *The Portable Financial Analyst* (Charlottesville, Va: The Association for Investment Management and Research, 1995, 54–55), modified duration is an accurate predictor of price change only for vanishingly small changes in yield to maturity. "If yield to maturity is 10 percent, for example, modified duration equals 6.14, which implies that a 100-basis-point change in yield to maturity will result in a 6.14 percent change in bond price. However, as yield to maturity increases to 10.25 percent, modified duration falls to 6.02, which implies smaller price changes for subsequent changes in yield to maturity. The price response of a bond to changes in yield to maturity is consequently a function not only of the bond's modified duration but of its convexity as well. Whereas modified duration measures the sensitivity of bond prices to changes in yield to maturity, convexity measures the sensitivity of duration to changes in yield to maturity."

3. For a full discussion of effective and other forms of duration, readers should refer to Frank J. Fabozzi's *Duration, Convexity, and Other Bond Risk Measures* (New York: John Wiley & Sons, Inc., 1999) and Mark Kritzman's *The Portable Financial Analyst* (Charlottesville, VA: The Association for Investment Management and Research, 1995).

CHAPTER 9

1. Frank J. Fabozzi, *The Handbook of Fixed Income Securities,* 7th edition (New York: McGraw-Hill, 2005).

CHAPTER 10

1. The Treasury auctions 2-year securities each month. The 12-month moving average adds the last 12-month yields at issuance and divides by 12. This provides the minimum market rate of return expected by this practitioner.

INDEX

Agency bonds, U.S., xv, xx, 20–21,
      26, 64–72, 78, 84
   Bloomberg on, 125–30, 143
   bullet, 123, 128–30, 141–42, 145
   callable, xx, 68, 71–72, 121–43,
      159
   losses and, 56, 100–101, 103–5
   politically correct portfolios and,
      36, 42–43, 47
   price fluctuation strategy and,
      66–67
   public fund analytics and,
      145–46, 156, 159
   risks and, 21, 53, 64–65, 68–69,
      71–72
American (continuous) structure,
      123–27, 136–43
amortizing, amortized cost, 54,
      96–97
Association of Public Treasurers of
      the United States and Canada,
      15–16, 36
average life, 111–14, 159
   durations vs., xx, 107–8, 111–13,
      120
   price volatility measurement
      and, xx, 107–11, 113–14,
      120

and time value of money,
      112–13

basis points, basis point changes,
      41, 66, 100, 119
   callable securities and, 128,
      134–35, 139
   durations and, 110, 115
   losses and, 58, 103–4
   opportunity costs and, 85–86, 88
   public fund analytics and,
      145–46, 150, 153
Bermuda (discrete) structure,
      123–24, 127, 132–33, 136–
      143
bid/offer spreads, 21, 69
   callable securities and, 135–38
   public fund analytics and,
      145–46
Bloomberg, 125–30, 143–44
bonds, bondholders, 16, 50, 78, 85,
      88–90, 106–11, 130
   corporate, xvi–xvii, 36–37, 41,
      53, 63–64, 69, 72, 145, 156
   discount, 95–99, 106, 109, 118
   durations and, 107–11, 114–18,
      120
   liquidity and, 21, 23

bonds, bondholders (*cont.*)
losses and, 52–54, 100–101,
103–4
par, 95–97, 99
performance appraisals and, 8–9,
25–26, 28–30
politically correct portfolios and,
36–41, 47–49
premium, 95–99, 106, 109
public fund analytics and, 145,
151–53, 156–60
risks and, 53, 63–69, 72, 99
Wall Street investing and, 4, 6
YTM and, 97–99, 118–19
see also Agency bonds, U.S.;
callable securities; Treasuries,
U.S.; zero coupons
budgets, budgeting, xiii, xv, 4, 17,
54–60, 96, 98–99, 122
callable securities and, 132–35,
142
durations and, 116–18
investment plans and, 20, 102
losses and, xx, 54–59, 101–3,
106
performance appraisals and,
25–27, 31–32
politically correct portfolios and,
36, 39, 41, 45–47, 49
political trade-offs and, 69–70
public fund analytics and,
149–52, 160
returns and, 91–94, 106
risks and, 60, 67, 69
volatility and, 11–12
YTM and, 119–20

callable securities, 88, 108, 120–43
anatomy of, 122–25
bid/offer spreads and, 135–38
Bloomberg on, 125–30, 143
bullets and, xx, 140–42
call structures of, 123–28, 132,
136–43
cash and, 130–31, 135–38,
141–43
durations and, xx, 133–35,
141–42
fixed coupon, 123, 128–29
income and, 121, 131–37,
139–43
lockout periods of, 124–27, 129,
132–43
Main Street investing and, 122,
131–35, 142–43
politically correct portfolios and,
37, 41
public fund analytics and,
151–53, 156, 159–61
recommendations on, 142–43
risks and, xx, 41, 67–68, 71–72,
130–36, 139, 141–43
set-up coupon, 123, 128–30
values and, 122, 130–31, 135–43
canary callables, 123–24, 128–29
Capital Ideas (Bernstein), 4–5
cash, cash flows, cash management,
xvii, 18, 66, 68, 96–100
average life and, 112–13
callable securities and, 130–31,
135–38, 141–43
discount bonds and, 97, 99
durations and, 109, 111, 113–18,
120
GIPs and, 61, 63
losses and, 55, 100, 104
opportunity costs and, 85, 88
and pain created by gains,
92–93, 106
par bonds and, 97, 99
performance appraisals and, 9,
32

politically correct portfolios and, xix, 39, 44–46

premium bonds and, 97–98

public fund analytics and, 146–49, 151, 153, 158, 161

YTM and, 118–20

see also liquidity

communication, xx, 12–13, 39, 56, 78, 89

constant maturity treasury (CMT), 149–50

continuous (American) structure, 123–27, 136–43

credit ratings, 62, 133, 155

caveat about published, 64

risks and, 21, 64–65, 72

defaults, 37, 72

callable securities and, 132–33

losses and, 52–53

deficits, 45–46, 147–48

disbursements, *see* obligation payments

discount rate, 112

discrete (Bermuda) structure, 123–24, 127, 132–33, 136–43

diversification, xvi, 4, 16–17, 50, 61–64

lack of, 61–63

performance appraisals and, 28, 30–32, 34

politically correct portfolios and, 39, 43–44

risks and, 21, 23, 30, 53, 64, 73

suitability and, 28, 30–31, 34

dollar, 66, 112–13, 117

durations, 20, 66, 107–20

average life vs., xx, 107–8, 111–13, 120

calculation of, 107–8

callable securities and, xx, 133–35, 141–42

cash flows and, 109, 111, 113–18, 120

definitions of, 107, 110, 114–15

effective, xx, 115, 120, 155–56, 159, 161

Macaulay, 115

modified, 110–11, 114–15, 120

politically correct portfolios and, 37, 48

in portfolio decisions, 115–18

prices and, xx, 107–11, 113–18, 120

public fund analytics and, 150, 155–56, 159, 161

YTMs and, 108–9, 115–16, 118–20

DV01, 66

earnings, *see* returns

European (one-time) structure, 123–24, 127–28, 136–37, 139–43

Fannie Mae, 126–27

federal funds rate, 117, 150

Federal Home Loan Bank (FHLB), 126–29, 132–35

Federal Home Loan Mortgage Corporation (FHLMC) (Freddie Mac), 128–29

and profiting from losses, 100–101, 103–4

Federal Reserve (Fed), 15, 117, 150

fiduciary benchmarks, xix, 25

fiscal emergencies, 6, 12, 25, 30, 43

"Five *We*'s of Suitability, The," 28–34

fixed-income securities, *see* bonds,
  bondholders
forecasts, forecasting, xvii, 56, 69,
  85, 94
  politically correct portfolios and,
    38, 41, 46
  public fund analytics and, 144,
    146, 149–53, 157, 161
  variances from, 38–39, 46
Future Income Forecasting tool,
  153, 161

gains, *see* returns
General Electric, 21
Governmental Accounting
  Standards Board (GASB 31),
    xvi, 71, 96–97
  callable securities and, 131–34
  durations and, 117, 133
  getting past, 56–59
  losses and, 54–59, 73, 83, 85–86,
    89, 96, 117, 132, 134
  mark-to-market and, 96
  opportunity costs and, 83–87, 89
  politically correct portfolios and,
    37, 39, 47
  selecting maturities and, 77–78
  volatility and, 12, 131, 133
Government Finance Officers
  Association (GFOA), 15–16,
    26, 32, 36
government investment pools
  (GIPs):
  overconcentration in, 61–63, 73
  public fund analytics and,
    152–53

*Handbook of Fixed Income Securities,
  The* (Fabozzi), 108, 121
Horizon Required Yield Analysis,
  153

income, *see* returns
income portfolios, 43–44, 46–49
inflation, 15, 61, 117
interest, interest rates, xv, 61,
  86–88, 90–93, 96–120,
    126–36
  callable securities and, 123,
    126–30, 132, 134–36, 139–40,
    142
  discount bonds and, 97–99
  durations and, xx, 108–11,
    113–18
  losses and, xx, 53, 57–58,
    100–106
  opportunity costs and, 84, 86–87
  and pain created by gains,
    91–93, 106
  performance appraisals and,
    27–30
  politically correct portfolios and,
    36–39, 48
  political trade-offs and, 69–70
  premium bonds and, 97–98
  price volatility and, 113–14
  public fund analytics and, 146,
    150–53, 155–57, 159, 161
  risks and, xx, 5, 22, 27–29, 32,
    34, 37, 48, 63–71, 78–79, 83,
    99, 104, 107, 109, 111–14,
    116, 118, 122, 131–34,
    141–43, 155–56
  sensitivity analysis and, 156–57
  and time value of money,
    112–13
  Wall Street investing and, 5–6
  YTM and, 118–20
internal rate of return (IRR),
  118
investment plans, 16–23, 86
  characteristics of, 17–18,
    20–23

comparisons between
investment policy and, 18–20,
23, 42
creating of, 36, 42
losses and, 53, 102
politically correct portfolios and,
35–36, 41–42, 47–49
public fund analytics and, 144,
151–52, 154–57, 159–61
reordering priorities of, 22
transition from investment
policy to, xix, 16–20
Investment Plan Status Reports,
154–57, 161
investment policies, 13–23, 62, 88,
122
characteristics of, 15–18, 21–23
comparisons between
investment plans and, 18–20,
23, 42
as framework for investing,
14–16
losses and, 52, 58, 60, 95
optimizing income and, 50–52
performance appraisals and, 8,
16, 25, 27, 31–32
politically correct portfolios and,
36, 42–43, 46–47, 49
prototypes for, 16
public fund analytics and, 144,
146, 149, 154–58, 160–61
reordering priorities of, 22
risk and, 15, 17–18, 21, 58
suitability and, 20, 35, 49
transition to investment plans
from, xix, 16–20
investment strategies, 27, 70,
88–91, 111
buy-and-hold, 16, 40–42,
90–91, 122, 151–52
callable securities and, 132–35

investment plans and, 16–18
investment tactics vs., 88
opportunity costs and, 85–86,
88
passive, 11–12, 41–42, 49, 65,
122, 151
public fund analytics and,
151–52, 159–60
risks and, 59, 65, 67
trading and, 11–12, 16, 40–41,
49, 57–58, 91, 94, 122, 135,
146, 151
volatility and, 11–12

laddering, 77–79, 142
Las Vegas Review-Journal, 51
legality, xix, 16–20
investment plans and, 17–19,
23
investment policies and, 16,
18–19, 47, 49
performance appraisals and, 28,
31, 34
politically correct portfolios and,
35, 47, 49
suitability and, 19–20, 28, 31, 34
liquidity, xiii, xviii–xix, 3–8, 70, 131
appropriate levels of, xix, 43–46,
50, 146–49, 152, 155–57,
161
callable securities and, 121, 136
different meanings of, 21
GIPs and, 61–63
investment plans and, 17–20,
22–23, 42, 86
investment policies and, 16,
19–23, 43, 58
losses and, 21, 23, 58, 99–100,
102
Main Street investing and, 3–4,
6–7, 13, 21

liquidity (*cont.*)
  opportunity costs and, 84, 86
  optimizing income and, 43,
    50–51
  performance appraisals and, 8,
    10, 24–25, 27–28, 31–34
  politically correct portfolios and,
    xix, 37–38, 41–46, 49
  portfolios for, xix, 43–45, 50,
    62–63, 68, 136, 146, 148–49,
    158
  public fund analytics and,
    145–49, 152, 155–58, 161
  risks and, 21, 37, 50, 61, 67–68,
    145
  selecting maturities and, 77–78
  suitability and, 28, 34
Liquidity Estimator tool, 146–49,
    152, 161
Local Agency Investment Fund
    (LAIF), 61–62, 152–53
losses, 82–83, 91, 94–97, 122
  budgeting and, xx, 54–59,
    101–3, 106
  callable securities and, 132,
    134–35
  communication and, 13, 56,
    89
  durations and, 116–17
  GASB and, 54–59, 73, 83,
    85–86, 89, 96, 117, 132, 134
  GIPs and, 62–63
  liquidity and, 21, 23, 58,
    99–100, 102
  Main Street investing and, 6, 52
  maturities and, 53–58, 77–78,
    95, 100–105
  opportunity costs and, 83,
    85–86, 89
  performance appraisals and, 25,
    28–29, 32, 55

  politically correct portfolios and,
    36–37, 39, 43–44
  political trade-offs and, 69–
    70
  premium bonds and, 96–97
  price fluctuation strategy and,
    66–67
  profiting from, xx, 94–96,
    99–106, 159
  public fund analytics and,
    159–60
  realized, 53–59, 66, 73, 85, 94,
    96, 99–101, 104–5, 160
  rebalancing and, xx, 57, 99,
    102–6
  recognized, 53–59, 66, 73, 96,
    134
  returns and, xx, 50, 52–60, 73,
    94–95, 99–106
  risks and, 52, 56, 58, 68, 101–2,
    104, 132
  unrealized, 53–60, 66–68, 73,
    78, 83, 85–86, 89, 94, 96, 117,
    132, 134

Main Street investing, 118
  callable securities and, 122,
    131–35, 142–43
  losses and, 6, 52
  performance appraisals and, 4–5,
    25
  political trade-offs and,
    69–70
  public fund analytics and, 145,
    150–51, 157
  returns and, xix–xx, 3–7, 12–13,
    51, 91–92
  Wall Street vs., xiii–xiv,
    xvii–xviii, 3–8, 12–13, 16,
    21, 52, 57, 69–70, 91, 99,
    122, 131, 145, 150–51

Main Street Optimization
  Framework (MSOF), 157–61
market, markets, xvi, 18–19,
  21–23, 79, 86, 89–92, 94–96,
  98–102
  callable securities and, 122,
    130–31, 134, 140
  cycles of, 15, 48, 94–95, 99–100
  durations and, 108, 111, 115,
    117–18
  GASB and mark-to-, 96
  GIPs and, 62–63
  investment policies and, 15, 23
  losses and, 53–58, 73, 94–95,
    99–102, 106
  and pain created by gains,
    91–92, 106
  performance appraisals and, 26,
    28–32
  politically correct portfolios and,
    38–39, 41–42, 48–49
  political trade-offs and, 69–70
  price volatility and, 113–14
  public fund analytics and,
    144–46, 149–53, 155–59,
    161
  risks and, 22, 41, 64–66, 68–69
  yields and, 100–102
marketability, see bid/offer
  spreads
market benchmarks:
  and Main Street vs. Wall Street
    investing, 5, 13
  performance appraisals and, xvii,
    xix, 8–9, 16, 24–25, 27, 32
  public fund analytics and,
    149–51, 161
market rate of return, xiii, 122
  forecasting of, 149–52, 157, 161
  and Main Street vs. Wall Street
    investing, 3–5

and performance appraisals, 28,
  31–34
and public fund analytics,
  149–52, 157–61
and suitablity, 28, 31–34
total returns vs., 31–33
Market Rate of Return Forecast
  tool, 151, 161
maturities, 6, 22–23, 62–66, 69, 85,
  91–105
  callable securities and, 122,
    124–29, 131–33, 136–39,
    141–42
  durations and, 108–11, 114–
    118
  investment policies and, 16,
    20
  long vs. short, 114
  losses and, 53–58, 77–78, 95,
    100–105
  optimal, 77, 88
  performance appraisals and, 8–9,
    25–26, 28–31
  politically correct portfolios and,
    37–43, 48–49
  public fund analytics and, 145,
    149–53, 156, 159–61
  returns and, 50, 77–80, 91–94
  risks and, 22, 63–65, 77–80
  selecting of, 77–81
  Treasuries and, 78–80, 122–23,
    132–33, 141
  see also yield to maturity
Merrill Lynch, 79
Merrill Lynch 1–3 Year
  Government Index, xix, 5,
  8–9, 24, 27, 32
money market investments, xv,
  42–43
  GIPs and, 61–63
  unrealized losses and, 54, 58

mortgage-backed securities (MBSs), 37, 41, 62, 111, 115, 121
mutual funds, xvi–xvii, 4, 10

net asset values (NAVs), 61

obligation payments, 18–21, 60, 93–94, 96, 99, 137
  in investment policies vs. investment plans, 18–20
  liquidity and, 21, 23
  losses and, 58, 102–3
  performance appraisals and, 25, 28
  politically correct portfolios and, 37–38, 44–45
  public fund analytics and, 146–49, 155, 161
one-time (European) structure, 123–24, 127–28, 136–37, 139–43
opportunity costs, xx, 83–89
optimization worksheets, 158–59
options, xx, 123–28, 132, 137–40
Orange County, Calif., 15, 43, 51, 132
  GASB and, 54–55
  GIP of, 62–63

perfect storm scenarios, 45–46, 147–49
performance appraisals, xvii–xix, 8–13, 24–34, 81–84
  communication and, 12–13
  and comparisons between fund managers, 8–11, 24, 26, 29
  creating new standard for, 28–33
  diversification and, 28, 30–32, 34

investment policies and, 8, 16, 25, 27, 31–32
legality and, 28, 31, 34
liquidity and, 8, 10, 24–25, 27–28, 31–34
losses and, 25, 28–29, 32, 55
Main Street investing and, 4–5, 25
market benchmarks and, xvii, xix, 8–9, 16, 24–25, 27, 32
and market rate of return, 28, 31–34
opportunity costs and, 84, 86–88
problems with current, 25–27
risks and, 8, 12, 25–30, 32–34, 81–83
total returns in, 25–27, 31, 33
see also public fund analytics
Performance Enhancement Table (PET), 87–88
politically correct portfolios:
  creating of, xix, 35–49
  investment plans and, 35–36, 41–42, 47–49
  liquidity and, xix, 37–38, 41–46, 49
  management styles and, 36, 40–42, 48–49
  returns and, xix, 35–44, 46–49, 59–60
  risks and, 35–41, 43, 46, 48–49, 61, 63
  safety and, 35–36, 38–40, 42–44, 49
  virtual, 43–44, 49
political trade-offs, 69–71, 73, 87
portfolios:
  creating of, 22–23, 25, 70
  optimizing of, 157–61
  structures of, 155–56

Portfolio Sensitivity Analysis, 156–57

price, prices, 21, 61
  callable securities and, 131–35, 142
  discount bonds and, 96–98
  durations and, xx, 107–11, 113–18, 120
  losses and, 56, 66–67, 95, 100–102
  par bonds and, 96–97, 99
  politically correct portfolios and, 40–41, 44, 47–49
  premium bonds and, 95–97
  public fund analytics and, 146, 158–59
  returns and, 91, 94
  risks and, 10, 66–67, 109–10, 116–17, 134–35, 150
  strategy for dealing with, 66–67
  volatility of, xx, 107–11, 113–14, 116, 118, 120, 131, 133–35, 141

principal, 7–9, 82, 94–97, 117
  average life and, 107, 111
  callable securities and, 130–32, 135, 142–43
  economic, 46, 59–61, 69–70, 72–73, 91–93, 102, 143
  investment policy and, 16, 21–23, 58, 95
  liquidity and, 22–23
  losses and, 53, 57–58, 94–96, 101–3, 105
  and Main Street vs. Wall Street investing, 3–4, 7, 13
  opportunity costs and, 84, 87, 89
  optimizing income and, xix–xx, 50–51
  and pain created by gains, 91–93

performance appraisals and, 24–25, 28, 32–33
political, 59–61, 69–73, 91–93, 96, 100, 105, 117
politically correct portfolios and, xix, 35, 37, 40, 43–44, 49
political trade-offs and, 69–70, 73
premium bonds and, 95–98
preservation of, xiv, xvii–xix, 3–5, 7–9, 13, 16, 21–25, 27–28, 32–33, 35, 40, 49–51, 58, 66, 73, 95–96, 101–3, 105, 122
price fluctuation strategy and, 66–67
public fund analytics and, 157, 160
risks and, 21–23, 46, 59–61, 64, 67–68, 71–72, 143
probabilities, 79–82, 132
profits, profiting, 40
  from losses, xx, 94–96, 99–106, 159
  unrealized losses and, 53, 96
public fund analytics, xx, 144–61
  forecasting future income and, 151–53, 157, 161
  Investment Plan Status Reports and, 154–57, 161
  liquidity and, 146–49, 152, 155–58, 161
  and market rate of return, 149–52, 157–61
  MSOF and, 157–61
  relative value and, 145–46, 161
public fund management, public fund managers:
  comparisons between, 8–13, 23–24, 26, 29, 82–83, 85–87, 92–93

public fund management, public
fund managers (*cont.*)
dilemmas of, 6–7, 43
expertise of, 39, 135
fiduciary responsibilities of,
35–36, 44, 51, 86
prudence of, 51–52, 60, 65, 69,
116, 150
stewardship role of, 46, 70, 122
public funds, public fund investing:
goals of, xiii–xiv, xvii–xx, 3–5,
7–9, 13, 24–25, 36
investment committees and
boards of, 39–40, 46, 53–54,
78, 84–85, 87–89, 102–3, 105,
148
transferring tools used in
individual investing to,
xvi–xvii, 4
uniqueness of, 26, 49
public services, 51–52, 87

rebalancing, 137
losses and, xx, 57, 99, 102–6
politically correct portfolios and,
41–42, 49
public fund analytics and, 151,
158–60
rebalancing worksheets, 159–60
reinvestment, reinvesting, 85, 88,
90, 94, 152
durations and, 117–18
losses and, xx, 57, 101, 104–5
and pain created by gains, 92,
106
politically correct portfolios and,
37, 40, 42
premium bonds and, 98–99
risks and, 37, 60, 67–72, 99, 122,
131–36, 141–42
YTM and, 119–20

return pickups, 100
returns, xiii–xx, 3–13, 22–33,
77–89, 91–106
callable securities and, xx,
121–22, 130–37, 139–43
communication and, 13, 89
durations and, 116–17
economic principal and, 60, 73,
91–93, 102
forecasting and, 151–53, 157,
161
investment plans and, 17, 22, 42,
102
investment policies and, xix,
15–17, 19, 22, 42–43, 58, 60,
95
losses and, xx, 50, 52–60, 73,
94–95, 99–106
Main Street investing and,
xix–xx, 3–7, 12–13, 51, 91–92
maturities and, 50, 77–80, 91–94
opportunity costs and, xx, 83–88
optimizing income and, xiv,
xviii–xx, 35, 37, 43, 46–47,
50–73, 89, 105
and pain created by gains,
91–94, 106
performance appraisals and,
8–10, 16, 24–33, 81–83
politically correct portfolios and,
xix, 35–44, 46–49, 59–60
political principal and, 60, 73,
91–93
premium bonds and, 95,
97–98
price fluctuation strategy and,
66–67
public fund analytics and, xx,
146, 149–53, 156–58, 160–61
realized gains and, 93–94
recognized gains and, 92, 94

risks and, xvii, xix–xx, 5–6,
12–13, 15, 17, 33, 35, 39, 46,
48, 50, 52, 56, 60, 64–65,
67–69, 71–72, 79–80, 83–85,
87–89, 104, 136, 139, 150, 158
seeking income and, 46–49
standard deviations and, 79–82
suboptimizing of, 83–85, 87
suitability and, 35, 51
Treasury bullets and, 141–42
unrealized gains and, 92, 94
volatility and, 11–12, 29
YTMs and, 118, 120
see also market rate of return;
profits, profiting; total
returns
risk, risks, xiii–xv, xvii–xx, 4–8,
58–73, 96, 107–18, 121–22
ability to take, 36–39
average life and, 111–14
callable securities and, xx, 41,
67–68, 71–72, 130–36, 139,
141–43
communication and, 12–13,
89
comparisons between, 64–65,
70–72, 132–35
credit, 5, 37, 41, 53, 63–67,
70–73, 84, 104, 108–11, 115,
122, 131–34, 141, 145, 155,
161
diversification and, 21, 23, 30,
53, 64, 73
durations and, xx, 108–11,
115–17, 133
GIPs and, 62–63
interest rates and, xx, 5, 22,
27–29, 32, 34, 37, 48, 63–71,
78–79, 83, 99, 104, 107, 109,
111–14, 116, 118, 122,
131–34, 141–43, 155–56

investment plans and, 17, 102
investment policies and, 15,
17–18, 21, 58
liquidity, 21, 37, 50, 61, 67–68,
145
losses and, 52, 56, 58, 68, 101–2,
104, 132
and Main Street vs. Wall Street
investing, xiii–xiv, 5–8, 12–13
maturities and, 22, 63–65, 77–
80
minimizing of, xvii, xix, 52–53,
59–61, 69, 73
opportunity costs and, xx,
84–85, 87–88
performance appraisals and, 8,
12, 25–30, 32–34, 81–83
political, xviii–xix, 5–8, 12–13,
36, 39–40, 46, 64, 67, 70–72,
101, 130–32, 135, 141, 143
politically correct portfolios and,
35–41, 43, 46, 48–49, 61, 63
political trade-offs and, 70, 73
portfolio structure and, 155–56
prices and, 10, 66–67, 109–10,
116–17, 134–35, 150
principal and, 21–23, 46, 59–61,
64, 67–68, 71–72, 143
public fund analytics and, xx,
145, 149–50, 155–56, 158,
161
reinvestment, 37, 60, 67–72, 99,
122, 131–36, 141–42
returns and, xvii, xix–xx, 5–6,
12–13, 15, 17, 33, 35, 39, 46,
48, 50, 52, 56, 60, 64–65,
67–69, 71–72, 79–80, 83–85,
87–89, 104, 136, 139, 150,
158
standard deviations and, 79–80,
150, 158

risk, risks (*cont.*)
  suitability and, 28–29, 34,
    36–40
  volatility and, 10, 12, 67, 114
  willingness to take, 36, 39–40

safety, xv–xvii, 7–8, 21–25, 63–64,
    69, 72–73
  callable securities and,
    121–22
  investment plans and, 22, 42
  investment policies and, xix, 16,
    19, 22, 43, 58
  losses and, 54, 58, 73, 101
  and Main Street vs. Wall Street
    investing, 3–5, 7, 13
  opportunity costs and, 83–84
  optimizing income and, xix–xx,
    43, 50–51
  performance appraisals and, 8,
    16, 24–25, 27–28, 31–33
  politically correct portfolios and,
    35–36, 38–40, 42–44, 49
  public fund analytics and, 146,
    157, 161
  risks and, 21–22, 61, 64
security selection, 73
  durations and, 115–16
  maturities and, 77–81
  politically correct portfolios and,
    40, 47–49
  public fund analytics and,
    157–61
  risks and, 60–61
self-examination, 48–49
sensitivity analysis, 156–57
Standard & Poor's (S&P), xvi, 62,
    64
standard deviations, 79–82, 150,
    158
stocks, xvi–xvii, 4, 21, 40, 130

suitability, xix, 22–23
  comparisons between legality
    and, 19–20
  five aspects of, 28–34
  investment plans and, 19–20
  investment policies and, 20, 35,
    49
  performance appraisals and,
    27–34
  politically correct portfolios and,
    35, 49
  and profiting from losses,
    99–100, 106
  public fund analytics and, 145,
    155–57
  returns and, 35, 51

taxes, taxpayers, xiii, xv–xvi, xviii,
    12, 78, 95–96, 105
  losses and, 55–56, 95
  and Main Street vs. Wall Street
    investing, 4, 6–7
  opportunity costs and, xx, 83,
    85, 87–89
  optimizing income and, xx,
    51–52
  performance appraisals and,
    9–10
total returns, xvii, 40, 99, 120, 122,
    135
  market rate of return vs., 31–33
  in performance appraisals,
    25–27, 31, 33
  public fund analytics and, 146,
    150–51, 157, 159
  of Treasuries, 79–80, 85
  unrealized losses and, 57–58
trade-offs, 157–58
  callable securities and, 131, 135,
    138–39, 143
  political, 69–71, 73, 87

risk vs. return, xx, 65, 71, 79–80, 84–85, 87–89, 139, 150, 158
Treasuries, U.S., xv, 62, 64–69, 92, 131–35
  bullet, 140–42
  callable securities and, 122, 132–35, 140–42
  durations and, 108–11, 115–18, 141
  investment plans and, 17, 20
  losses and, 53, 55–56, 58–59, 100–105
  maturities and, 78–80, 122–23, 132–33, 141
  opportunity costs and, 84–88
  performance appraisals and, 26, 28, 31–34
  politically correct portfolios and, 36–37, 41–43, 48
  premium bonds and, 97–98
  price volatility and, 113–14
  public fund analytics and, 145–46, 149–50, 156
  risks and, 22, 53, 64–65, 67–69, 71, 141
  standard deviations and, 79–80, 82
  total return analysis of, 79–80, 85

underwriters, 125–29

value, values, 90–92, 110–15, 117–18
  average life and, 112–13
  callable securities and, 122, 130–31, 135–43
  discount bonds and, 96, 98
  durations and, 110–11, 115, 117
  lockouts and, 140–41
  losses and, 53–54, 56–58, 100–103, 105
  of one dollar, 112–13
  opportunity costs and, 83, 86
  of options, 137–40
  and pain created by gains, 91–92
  performance appraisals and, 26, 28–32
  politically correct portfolios and, 38–42, 49
  political trade-offs and, 69–70
  premium bonds and, 96, 98
  price volatility and, 113–14
  public fund analytics and, 145–46, 152, 155–56, 161
  relative, 145–46, 161
  risks and, 22, 63–66
  volatility and, 10–12
Vandals' Crown, The (Millman), 121
volatility, 66, 79, 150
  callable securities and, 131, 133–35
  in comparisons between funds, 10–12
  durations and, xx, 107–11, 114, 116, 118
  Main Street investing and, 5, 12
  performance appraisals and, 11, 29, 32–33, 81–82
  politically correct portfolios and, 36, 39, 41, 44
  of prices, xx, 107–11, 113–14, 116, 118, 120, 131, 133–35, 141
  returns and, 11–12, 29
  risks and, 10, 12, 67, 114
  unrealized losses and, 55, 57–58
volume changes, 40

Wall Street investing, 120
approach of, 4–7
Main Street vs., xiii–xiv,
xvii–xviii, 3–8, 12–13, 16, 21,
52, 57, 69–70, 91, 99, 122,
131, 145, 150–51
performance appraisals and, xix,
25–26
political trade-offs and, 69–70
public fund analytics and,
145–46, 150–51, 157, 159
returns and, 5, 91
value and, 131, 135
Wall Street Journal, xiii, 69
Washington Public Power Supply
System, 64
Wells Fargo, 126–27
worst-case scenarios, 86
politically correct portfolios and,
45–46
public fund analytics and, 147,
149

yields, 68–72, 79–80, 88, 92,
97–104
callable securities and, 122–23,
131–36, 138–43

durations and, 108–11, 114–16,
118–20
market, 100–102
performance appraisals and, xix,
25, 27, 31–32
politically correct portfolios and,
37, 48
and profiting from losses, 95,
99–104, 106
public fund analytics and, 145,
149–53, 158–61
purchase, 27, 100, 151–53, 158,
160
risks and, 21, 68–69, 71–72
take-out, 100–104, 106, 160
Treasuries and, 66, 69, 80,
97–98, 122–23, 132–35
yield to maturity (YTM), 97–100
and discount bonds, 97–99
and durations, 108–9, 115–16,
118–20
and premium bonds, 97–98
weakness of, 118–20

zero coupons, 65, 116–18
durations and, 108–9, 116–17
price volatility and, 113–14

ABOUT THE AUTHOR

Ben Finkelstein is the senior managing director of public funds for Stanford Group Company. He has spent more than a decade developing training programs specifically for public fund investment professionals and supervisors. In addition, he is a nationally recognized consultant, lecturer, and published author in the public funds investment community. Before joining Stanford Group Company, he served as a first vice president of institutional fixed income sales for Lehman Brothers' Capital Markets Group.

National organizations such as the Government Finance Officers Association, the Association of Public Treasurers of the United States and Canada, Public Risk Management Association, and Public Agency Risk Managers Association, as well as numerous state and local organizations, including the State of Missouri, Florida League of Cities, Florida GFOA, California Municipal Treasurers Association, and the California Society of Municipal Finance Officers, have all benefited from his lectures. Individual companies such as Bank of America and cities including St. Louis have had Mr. Finkelstein develop in-house training programs.

Mr. Finkelstein holds the Chartered Financial Analyst designation and is an active member in the Houston Society of Financial Analysts as well as the CFA Institute.

Stanford Group Company is a member of Houston-based Stanford Financial Group, a global network of affiliated financial companies headed by chairman and CEO R. Allen Stanford.